"Those we love have the ability to hurt us the most. This is the reality that we live in, but Pastor Jentezen, in his engaging way, has given us the tools to love through our pain. My friend has an inspired word from God that will enrich your life. Pick up a copy of his new book today."

Mark Batterson, pastor; *New York Times* bestselling author, *The Circle Maker*

"*Love Like You've Never Been Hurt* is a profound message on the power of unconditional love. A must-read for those ready to shed off the wounds of the past and sprint full force into the whole and abundant life God has planned. In Jentezen's words, 'Getting hurt is a part of life. It's inevitable. But that is not the end of the story.' It's time to start fresh, to heal, and to learn to love without bounds."

Lisa Bevere, *New York Times* bestselling author; co-founder, Messenger International

"This could be the most powerful book you read. Pastor Jentezen Franklin's new book, *Love Like You've Never Been Hurt*, shows us Christ's extravagant love and inspires us to love as God loved us. If you've been hurt, betrayed, disappointed or crushed, this book will strengthen your faith and renew your hope that you can love again."

Craig Groeschel, senior pastor, Life.Church; author, *Daily Power: 365 Days of Fuel for Your Soul*

# LOVE
### LIKE YOU'VE
### NEVER BEEN
# HURT

# LOVE
## LIKE YOU'VE NEVER BEEN
# HURT

### HOPE, HEALING
### AND THE
### POWER OF AN OPEN HEART

## JENTEZEN FRANKLIN
#### WITH CHERISE FRANKLIN
#### AND A. J. GREGORY

**Chosen**

*a division of Baker Publishing Group*
Minneapolis, Minnesota

Published by Chosen Books
11400 Hampshire Avenue South
Bloomington, Minnesota 55438
www.chosenbooks.com

Chosen Books is a division of
Baker Publishing Group, Grand Rapids, Michigan

Printed in the United States of America

Library of Congress Cataloging-in-Publication Data
Names: Franklin, Jentezen, author.
Title: Love like you've never been hurt : hope, healing, and the power of an open heart / Jentezen Franklin, with Cherise Franklin.
Description: Minneapolis, Minnesota : Chosen, 2018. | Includes bibliographical references.
Identifiers: LCCN 2017039155 | ISBN 9780800798642 (cloth : alk. paper)
Subjects: LCSH: Love—Religious aspects—Christianity. | Pain—Religious aspects—Christianity. | Suffering—Religious aspects—Christianity.
Classification: LCC BV4639 .F68 2018 | DDC 241/.4—dc23
LC record available at https://lccn.loc.gov/2017039155

ISBN 978-0-8007-9864-2 (cloth)
ISBN 978-0-8007-9865-9 (ITPE)

Cover design by LOOK Design Studio

Author is represented by The FEDD Agency, Inc.

18  19  20  21  22  23  24          8  7  6  5  4  3

To our grandchildren, Amelia and Luca,
that they might live out a legacy of mercy and love.

# CONTENTS

# ACKNOWLEDGMENTS

Thank you:

To my amazing wife, Cherise, who has walked every step of this book with me. May the lessons in these chapters leave a legacy of grace, love and forgiveness to our five wonderful children: Courteney, Caressa, Caroline, Connar and Drake.

To A. J. Gregory. This book would not have been possible without your tremendous contribution. You're the best, and it has been an honor working with you.

To Esther Fedorkevich and the wonderful staff at The Fedd Agency for seeing this project through from start to finish.

To the Free Chapel family and those individuals who have labored to make this work possible.

To Kim Bangs and the dedicated team at Chosen for believing in this book.

# INTRODUCTION

Mark Twain said, "If you pick up a starving dog and make him prosperous, he will not bite you. This is the principal difference between a dog and a man."[1] Twain was right.

You can care for a dog that has been abused. You can love it. You can nurture it. You can feed it. You can call it your own. Despite the pain that this animal has endured and because of your love for it, this dog will become your best friend. He will greet you at the door every day. He will come when you call. And he will be loyal to you until his dying day.

As true as this mutually sacrificial relationship is of dogs, it is not always true of human beings. In fact, I believe the very people we love the most will hurt us the most.

We have to learn how to love like we've never been hurt.

This is critical because, as sure as you are reading this book, someone is going to break your heart. Someone is going to abandon you or leave you. Someone is going to say something hurtful to you. Someone is going to disappoint you. Someone is going to let you down, lie to you, stab you in the back. Someone is going to reject you.

Chances are, someone already has. As you read these words, you may be picturing the face of the person who has caused you pain. The parent who left home when you were five years old. The spouse who cheated on you. The sibling who refuses to talk to you. The child who has chosen to rebel. The friend who betrayed a sacred secret.

Whatever it is, you have loved hard and were wounded. This someone has cut off your love supply. And you are not living fully, the way God intended, because you do not know how, or if it is even possible, to love like you've never been hurt.

It's easy to love others when we have no conflict with them. Or when we share the same viewpoints. Or the same theology. Or the same standard. It's easy to love when marriage is in the honeymoon stage, when our children act right all the time, when we have our health and our happiness.

But no one lives in that kind of state all the time.

Jesus told us that in this world we would have trouble (John 16:33). In Matthew 18:7 (NKJV), He even says, "Offenses must come."

Getting hurt is part of life. It's inevitable. But that is not the end of the story.

God does not want us to be the walking wounded. He intended for us to be healed and to be whole. He created us to love like we've never been hurt because that is what He does, and we are made in His image.

James Garfield had been the twentieth president of the United States for only four months when he was shot in the back on July 2, 1881, by a would-be assassin. He lived just under three months more.

You would think it was the shot that killed him. It wasn't.

You see, the bullet did not penetrate any vital organs. It got stuck behind his pancreas, but it was not a fatal injury. But back then, doctors weren't concerned about germs; they did not even believe they existed because they couldn't see them. So minutes after President Garfield was shot, doctors pressed in around him to stick their fingers and push unsterilized instruments into his wound. They poked and prodded as far as they could in his body, hoping to find the bullet and remove it. They continued to do this for eighty days while President Garfield languished in the hospital. As we today would expect, this regular unsterilized digging worsened the president's condition. He developed infections and eventually died.

I find it fascinating that President Garfield did not succumb to death because of the bullet wound. He died from the infections caused by doctors who kept probing the wound.

Funny—we tend to do this with our own wounds. We replay the bad memories again and again. We talk about them repeatedly to anyone who will listen. We think of ways we can exact revenge. We poke and prod at our gaping wounds. In the process, we become bitter. Hardened. And, often, we withhold our love from those who need it most.

But this is not how God wants us to live. He wants to give us a new beginning. A new story. A fresh start. He wants to heal what has been broken. He wants to reconcile what has been torn apart.

This is about understanding biblical forgiveness and reconciliation and establishing healthy boundaries, as I will explain in this book. Love without limits is not about codependence or irrational thinking, and it is not an invitation to be used as a doormat or a whipping post.

The bottom line is that we need to put our relationships back together. The Body of Christ is full of parents who are estranged from their own children. Some of us have not spoken to family members in years, though they live only a few miles away. Some grandchildren have never even met their grandparents. Some Christians who were abused growing up still harbor the injustice, making it difficult to pursue healthy relationships in their own families.

Some have lost loved ones and are too hurt to figure out how to love the ones that are left.

This sickness can only be healed by Love.

> If I speak in the tongues of men and of angels, but have not love, I am only a resounding gong or a clanging cymbal. If I have the gift of prophecy and can fathom all mysteries and all knowledge, and if I have a faith that can move mountains, but have not love, I am nothing. If I give all I possess to the poor and surrender my body to the flames, but have not love, I gain nothing.
>
> Love is patient, love is kind. It does not envy, it does not boast, it is not proud. It is not rude, it is not self-seeking, it is not easily angered, it keeps no record of wrongs. Love does not delight in evil but rejoices with the truth. It always protects, always trusts, always hopes, always perseveres.
>
> 1 Corinthians 13:1–8

Love never fails.

Love is a powerful force. In this passage, Paul notes that our problem in the Church is that we place power gifts higher than love. But good preaching, revival services and prophetic words, without love, will fail. You can't win the lost with any other language than the language of love.

When we seek to love God, love ourselves and love others, we can learn to love despite what happened in the past. We can mend brokenness that has plagued our families for generations. In fact, Paul wrote in 2 Corinthians 5 that we are to have a ministry of reconciliation (see verse 18). If you are a believer in Jesus Christ, you are called to reconcile.

It is never wrong to love.

It is never out of order to love.

You do not compromise when you love.

You never lower your standards when you love.

I know these are loaded truths for some of you to digest, and I will unpack what they mean throughout this book. Many of us fail to realize that what matters most in life is relationships. An abundant life does not consist of the abundance of stuff. The world does not place much value on relationships. It tells us money is important. Titles are important. The right zip code is important. Looks are important. Fast cars and big homes are important.

Do you remember when Jesus was asked what the greatest commandment was? He replied, "'You shall love the LORD your God with all your heart, with all your soul, and with all your mind.' This is the first and great commandment. And the second is like it: 'You shall love your neighbor as yourself'" (Matthew 22:37–39 NKJV).

Here Jesus emphasized in a big way the importance of relationships. This is what life is about—loving God, loving ourselves and loving others.

I get what it's like to be hurt. I'm not telling you to do something I have not done myself—and even made mistakes along the way trying. I know the temptation to not want to let go of hurt or disappointment.

My marriage has had severe tests and struggles, and so has my family. In writing this book, my wife and I decided to share some things we have never shared before. We determined we don't have to keep up a ministerial front. Life gets real! At times I felt unqualified to preach to others because my own marriage and family were going through hell.

What I learned was if you're going through hell, don't stop there. Keep going 'til you get to the other side.

I have discovered that trouble is one of God's great servants because it reminds us how much we continually need Him. God is not put off by our struggles. He says, *I'll help you. I really will.* When you have gone as far as you can, you have just pulled up into God's driveway. When you are ready to throw up your hands, throw them up to Him.

Some moments change everything about you and your family for the rest of your life. Whether loss, a betrayal, an addiction, an infidelity—without a doubt, these things affect the dynamics of our relationships.

But God creates all things new.

It is time to let Him give you a new beginning. It is time to let God bind up your bruises and heal your wounds.

I love these words written by the ancient prophet:

> Moreover the light of the moon will be as the light of the sun, and the light of the sun will be sevenfold, as the light of seven days, in the day that the LORD binds up the bruise of His people and heals the stroke of their wound.
>
> Isaiah 30:26 NKJV

If you let God heal your wounded places, your nights will become like days and your days will shine seven times brighter.

Think about this for a moment.

Do you want to be right or reconciled?

Do you want to be hurt or healed?

Do you want to keep being the victim or start becoming whole?

Since you have started reading this book, I am pretty confident I know what you would answer. And the only way to be reconciled, healed and whole is to love like you've never been hurt.

# CHAPTER ONE

# LOVE MATTERS

Our daughter glared at my wife, Cherise, and me. Her eyes blazed with anger.

If you have ever raised a teenager, you know what I am talking about. I don't know what it is, but most kids at this age seem to lose their minds for about six years.

"You can't tell me what to do!" my daughter shouted.

I looked at her square in the face. "We're going to work this out."

"Ugh," she groaned. "No way! I'm out of here."

"Oh, no! You are not going anywhere until we sit down and talk!" I said with clenched teeth.

The second our daughter turned toward our bedroom door, I jumped into position. Fullback position. Stretching out each arm, I blocked her path.

"You can't trap me here!" our daughter yelled.

"Oh yes, we can," I shot back, my arms waving wildly.

My frustration mounted, but my heart broke. Arguments like this one had taken place many times, it seemed, not just with this daughter, but with others as well.

During that particular episode, we were smack in the middle of a family crisis. Each day brought another fight. Some clashes were more disruptive than others. Some aroused deep sadness. Others harsh words.

It started when our oldest daughter went off to college. Growing up, she was a model child. But during the first few weeks of school, away from home, she began to stray. She wanted to see what it was like on the other side of church life. She got involved with the wrong crowd. And she made some of the worst choices that a young girl could make.

As the situation grew more serious, my wife and I knew we had to do something.

I will never forget the day I was putting the final touches on a sermon I was about to preach in thirty minutes. Cherise flew into the room, on a mission. The look on her face said it all.

"Jentezen, I'm going to get our daughter. Are you going to choose the church and stay and preach, or are you going to choose your daughter and come with me?"

The answer was obvious. I dropped what I was doing to take care of my family.

Cherise and I did not speak much on the three-hour drive to the university. Our daughter did not know we were coming, let alone coming to pull her out of school and bring her home. We didn't know what to expect.

Once we arrived, Cherise phoned her. My wife asked what she was doing but did not mention we were there. I waited in the car while Cherise walked into the building where our daughter was. Suddenly, my wife saw her walking toward the lobby where she stood. The minute our daughter saw Cherise, she broke down. Collapsing to her knees, she began to sob uncontrollably.

"We're taking you home," Cherise said, gently. "Right now."

And with those words, the three of us drove off-campus. None of us looked back. We did not even go to our daughter's dorm and take anything with us; we left her room as is. The stuff did not matter. We wanted our baby girl home.

Once she settled back in with us, things got even worse in some ways. We begged and pleaded with her. We argued and screamed at her. We tried to control her with money. We took away her car. We forbade her to party and hang out with friends who were bad influences. Nothing worked. She just hardened more and more.

This constant contention began to affect the atmosphere of our home. We were always having arguments, confronting lies and deceptions. This crisis sucked the life out of my wife and me. Our hearts were broken. We felt little joy. We were different people, aged and emotionally exhausted.

At times Cherise and I disagreed on how we should discipline. This brought a friction into our marriage that was overwhelming. Satan's strategy has never changed: divide and conquer. A house divided cannot stand.

My other children were enduring life in this war zone. They noticed quickly the change that came over Cherise and me. And they did not like it. Three of our kids were teenagers at the time and had their own stuff to deal with. It seemed every day we were battling a crisis of some sort with at least one of our children.

> Satan's strategy has never changed: divide and conquer.

One such moment was the incident I wrote about at the beginning of this chapter. Let's get back to it for a moment. When I was blocking my daughter from leaving the room, I could not help but wonder, *When is this all going to end?*

The argument escalated. I noticed my voice getting louder and tried hard to tame my tongue. It was not easy. Our daughter tried to make another move toward the closed bedroom door, but Cherise and I were determined. We stood fast, blocking her every turn.

Exasperated, she finally yelled, "If you don't let me do what I want to do, I'm going to—" As she hurled a desperate and emotion-filled threat to harm herself, I shot back with words of my own. Of course, there was no legitimate truth to what she said—my wife and I knew it was typical teenage theatrics—but it was a tipping point that brought the dramatic exchange to full blast. All three of us were yelling at that point. The conversation was going nowhere, but the conflict was growing.

It went on like this for a while. At some point, Cherise left the room. When she stepped out into the hallway, she practically tripped over our two youngest children. Our youngest daughter was ten, and our youngest child and only son was nine. I cannot remember which one was doing what, but one of them was praying earnestly and the other pleading the blood of Jesus over and over. It was a tender moment.

As our daughter tells it, in overhearing the heated argument, she had taken it upon herself to run spiritual interference. She grabbed her brother from whatever he was doing and said, "You need to come with me to Mom and Dad's room quick. The devil is in the house. We've got to go down there and pray!"

Our son nodded and followed suit. "Hey," he piped up, as they dashed down the stairs to the first floor, "get the Bible. We need to take a Bible with us."

Midstride, our daughter bobbed her head in agreement and ran back up to her room. When our son saw her bolting back down the stairs with her girlie-pink Bible, his eyes went wide. "No, no, no!" he said, shaking his head. "A pink Bible's not going to work. The devil is *really* in this house! You've got to get a black Bible!"

Cherise and I burst out laughing when our daughter told us this story. It helped to take the edge off, briefly.

But even a cute story cannot mask a desperate reality.

The constant arguments and contention in our home fragmented our once-peaceful family dynamic. Strangely, as our family struggled to tread water and stay afloat, our church grew exponentially. Amazing doors began to open for the ministry. New multimillion-dollar buildings were built. My books became *New York Times* bestsellers. Christian TV networks began to broadcast our weekly sermons all over the world. All of this was happening while I was going through what felt like the valley of the shadow of death in my own home.

Looking back on how Cherise and I kept functioning, I can only say it was by the grace of God. Some Sundays, before I would preach, I would get on my knees in my office and just weep. "God," I would say, "I don't know how I'm going to do this. I'm afraid. I'm broken. I'm hurting. I feel like running away and never coming back. But I do not go in my name or my own power. I go in Your name and the power of Your Spirit. I will not give up the fight for my family. Help me. I belong to You. I'm Yours." And when I would stand up and preach, God's grace would come and the services would be powerful.

> God is attracted to weakness. When we are empty vessels, He longs to fill us with His grace, love and goodness.

I have discovered an astonishing truth: God is attracted to weakness. He cannot resist when we humbly and honestly admit how desperately we need Him. When we are empty vessels, He longs to fill us with His grace, love and goodness. This is God's law of attraction.

I remember countless Sundays during which our kids accompanied us to church but made clear it was the last place they wanted to be. Never underestimate the power of just being there. When it seems like the Word is not working, it is. If you will work the Word, the Word will work. It will not return void. Whatever bad news we would receive about our teenage girls, we would keep on interceding, keep on bringing them to church, keep on marching them into the front row. And I kept on preaching the Word.

One weekend, my wife called me. Our oldest daughter had left home. We had just returned from a trip to Orange County, California, to a note that she had left for good. It said something like, "I can't live by these rules. I'm going to do what I want to do. I can't keep causing you this pain." Cherise remembers thinking that at least our daughter was courteous enough to leave a note before taking off for the last time.

My wife and I were heartbroken. We did not know where she was for about a week. Cherise went into what could only be described as a grieving process. We did everything we could to find our daughter, and we could not. We mourned for days and nights, not knowing where our child was.

Finally, after about a week, she called. She reassured us that she was okay and that she was working as a nanny for a local family. For the next few months, she came around our home only on occasion. Our contact with her was very limited. One day, she told us she had fallen in love. Months later, she got married by a justice of the peace. We found out via a text.

It was a crushing blow to a family that was once very close. Cherise felt robbed of the dream of preparing for and watching our first daughter get married. I remember, a week later, officiating the wedding of one of her friends. When I watched the bride and her father walk down the aisle, my heart broke. I was devastated. It took everything in me not to show my emotion. I would never get that opportunity to do the same with my own daughter.

> Some things get broken and can never be put back exactly the same. Yet God can make all things new.

The truth is, some things get broken and can never be put back exactly the same. Yet God can make all things new.

It was at this time that I first heard the phrase *Love like you've never been hurt*. People speculate as to who said it originally, but the words came alive in my heart when I heard it.

If you will be willing to love like you've never been hurt, God can heal every broken relationship in your life. Nehemiah 4:2 talks about the Israelites rebuilding the walls of Jerusalem from dust and burned stones. "Do they actually think they can make something of stones from a rubbish heap—and charred ones at that?"

Do not throw away the stones that have been burned. God can and will use them to rebuild your family.

Reconnecting and rebuilding the broken walls in our family has not been an easy or quick process, I admit. We still have challenges that we have to work through and get over. But we have determined to love like we've never been hurt. It is a choice we have to make over and over and over again.

Now, we haven't always done it right, but Cherise and I have made this commitment to our family. We've been encouraged by the ancient proverb that says when you raise your children in the way that they should go, when they get older, they will not depart from it (see Proverbs 22:6).

Our oldest daughter today loves Jesus with all of her heart. She is the media director of a large church in the Atlanta area. Her husband works there also as a graphic artist. They blessed us with our first beautiful granddaughter, Amelia.

Another daughter is married and together with her husband pastors our church in Orange County and have a precious son, Luca. My third daughter went to Oral Roberts University, graduated from Vanguard University in California and is involved in ministry. My youngest daughter is in her second year of college in Los Angeles. She is a professional model and she loves Jesus supremely. Our son is a student at Liberty University and is pursuing a huge call on his life. This has been the fruit of refusing to allow hurt to dictate how we love our children.

As I was writing this chapter, I remembered the first sermon I ever preached. I was twenty years old. I pulled up to a little country church where I would speak in front of fifty people. As I approached the pulpit, nerves knotted my stomach.

I spoke from Philippians 3:13–14 (NKJV),

> I do not count myself to have apprehended; but one thing I do, forgetting those things which are behind and reaching forward to those things which are ahead, I press toward the goal for the prize of the upward call of God in Christ Jesus.

I stumbled through that message nervously. But when I concluded, God had touched lives and the altars were filled.

The biggest point in that first sermon was this: "You don't just need a good memory. Sometimes you need a good forgettery." To move forward, you have to let go of the past. You have to release what is behind you and reach for what is before you. If you will reach for a new day, God will begin, little by little, to release you from the past.

> **To move forward, you have to release the past and reach for the future.**

Funny, 34 years later, I am writing this book with a heavy mandate from God to say the same thing.

Life is an adventure in forgiveness. It is all about releasing and reaching. Release the past and reach for the future. The only way to do this is to love like you've never been hurt. This means loving so intensely that it overrides all your natural instincts for bitterness and revenge.

You will never get ahead trying to get even. When you have been wronged, a poor memory is your best response. A good forgettery is what all of us need.

Have you ever noticed how a jeweler shows his best diamonds? He sets them against a black velvet backdrop. The contrast of the jewels against the dark background accentuates their luster.

In the same way, God does His most stunning work where things seem hopeless. Wherever there is pain, suffering and desperation, Jesus is there. There is no better place for the brilliance of Christ to shine.

I do not know what is going on in your life as you read this book. But I do know this: The pain you feel today is the pain you can heal.

I have never felt the pain of addiction. I have never felt the pain of losing a child. I have never felt the pain of divorce. I can only offer people the advice of God's Word and prayer. But people who have *been through* those valleys and felt that pain are more qualified to help heal someone going through the same crisis. What is important to remember, however, is that regardless of the source of your pain, God can heal you.

It has been said that family provides us with life's greatest joys and at times life's deepest sorrows. When I think about how hard it is to make the family work, the challenges that come and the complications involved, it is really something else. Family members know how to tick us off. They can get on our nerves. The people we love most are the ones who potentially, through offenses, can infect us if we do not react right. But I have learned that with challenges comes opportunity. And family also provides the greatest opportunity for us to learn how to love like we've never been hurt.

## THE **BIG** IDEA

The pain you feel today is the pain you can heal.

# CHAPTER TWO

# LOVE NEVER FAILS

Many Christians these days do not know how to make their families work. The Body of Christ is full of parents estranged from their own children. Some of them have never even seen their grandchildren. Some folks have not picked up the phone and spoken with loved ones in years because of petty squabbles. Some Christians have written off family members just because they have chosen to live by a different standard.

Something's not right about this!

We just do not know how to love—all the time. Oh, we can love when we agree with one another. We can love when we share the same viewpoints. We can love when we share the same lifestyle. We can even love strangers or those who don't know us well. But it sure is harder to love those who are closest to us. Why? Because they can hurt us the most.

## Love Wins—All the Time

As believers, we are called to live differently. We do not love as the world loves, which is conditionally, only when expectations are met or when it feels good. We love God's way.

There are only two subjects in the Bible that God thinks are important enough to ascribe an entire chapter to: one, faith (see Hebrews 11), and two, love (see 1 Corinthians 13). Evidently, God feels that love and faith are so important they must be foundational truths in our lives.

God knows that love is a powerful weapon. When He looks at our world held captive by the enemy, He knows the way to fight is not with angels, prophetic words or powerful worship. His greatest weapon is love.

Love is kind. Love thinks no evil. Love is permanent. Love endures. Love does not give up. You cannot walk in love until you walk in forgiveness. We may not see eye to eye on everything, but if we focus on the blood and the forgiveness of Jesus Christ, we can have unity! We can love one another as God loves us.

After Jesus rose from the dead, He searched out and found His disciple Simon Peter. Then He asked him a question three times: "Simon, do you love me?" (John 21:15–17). In English, we have but one word for *love*. In the Greek language, however, there are three. *Eros* means "sexual." *Phileo* says, "I'm attracted to you. I feel something for you." But the highest level of love is *agape*, which is "divine love."

When Jesus asked Simon, "Do you *agape* Me?" He was asking, "Do you have the highest level of love for Me?" Simon answered, "I *phileo* You" ("I feel something for You"). In other words, he was not on the same level of love as what Jesus was asking for.

Jesus asked him again, "Do you *agape* Me? Do you have divine love for Me?" Simon Peter got a little riled at Jesus, and he said back to Him, "Yes, Lord! I *phileo* You!" The third time is the interesting one. Jesus asked, "Simon, do you *phileo* Me?"

In other words, Jesus offered him the highest level of love, and when he realized that Simon Peter could not match it, He brought it down a notch. I wonder, how many things would God do for us if we moved up a level in our love for Him? If we had more than a casual relationship with Him? If we gave Him free rein in our hearts?

I believe God is calling us to a new level of love.

Love is the answer to the broken home. Love is the answer to the addict. Love is the answer to fractured relationships. Love is the answer to being offended. Love is the answer to heartbreak. Love is a weapon that can shatter division and rebuild what has been broken.

What is happening in your life right now that tests you in the way you love? Did you just discover that your spouse has been cheating on you? Do you want to reconnect with the daughter you haven't spoken to in months? Did your son just tell you his girlfriend is pregnant? Is your teenager suffering from an addiction that is overwhelming not just his life but every single person in your family? Has your adult daughter declared she's a lesbian and she's done with the whole God business?

> **Love is a weapon that can shatter division and rebuild what has been broken.**

Different dynamics and complexities characterize each of these situations. But they're real. They're hard. And they hurt.

I wonder what would happen if we decided that, with God's help and in His strength, we are going to love like we've never been hurt. Instead of withholding affection, staying bitter or seeking revenge, we love.

And, once we have decided to do it, how? Through some key choices that will help us get there:

1. Choose love over hurt.
2. Choose to love others—always.

3. Choose to press forward.

4. Choose to heal your wounds.

5. Choose to keep driving.

## Choose Love over Hurt

The Bible gives us many examples of people who chose love over hurt. These people knew that love never fails.

I think about the young man Joseph. The second youngest of twelve brothers born to Jacob, he was his father's favorite, and everyone in the family knew it. Jealousy got the best of the brothers. They hated Joseph and could not speak a kind word to him (see Genesis 37:4).

Joseph also had a gift: the ability to interpret dreams. When he had a dream that his family bowed down to him, he blurted it out to his brothers, and their hatred of him swelled. They grew so jealous they devised a plan to murder him. But one of the brothers, Judah, suggested that instead of killing Joseph, it was better to sell him as a slave. Later, they tricked their father into believing the poor boy had been slain by a wild animal.

Think about this: Joseph was not abandoned by strangers. He was betrayed by family. His very own flesh and blood sold him like a filthy, good-for-nothing piece of trash.

Maybe you know well the sting of hatred or resentment. Maybe a close friend abandoned you because he or she was jealous. Instead of encouraging you, believing in you, this person cut you off. I want to remind you that when Joseph's world turned upside down, when all hope seemed dried up, he held on.

Carried far from home, Joseph was sold to an Egyptian official in Pharaoh's palace. Then he was falsely accused of rape and thrown in prison. While in prison, he correctly interpreted the dreams of some fellow prisoners, and eventually he was summoned by Pharaoh to interpret one of his dreams. It was not a good one. The dream meant that Egypt would experience seven years of prosperity followed by seven years of famine. Joseph also threw in some good advice for the Egyptian leader, suggesting that Pharaoh put someone in charge of the entire nation who would help gather food produced in the good years and store it away (Genesis 41:33–36). Pharaoh was so moved that he appointed Joseph to be second-in-command over Egypt.

During the famine, Joseph's older brothers came to Egypt to buy food. They stood in front of the brother they had sold, but they could not recognize him. Joseph was a powerful man. He held the keys to the world's food supply. And before him stood the very family members who abused him and allowed him to serve thirteen years as a slave and to be put in prison for a crime he did not commit.

Joseph had a choice.

He could either give them as good as they gave him, or he could love like he had never been hurt.

It has been said that the depth of your hurt determines the width of your response. When you have been hurt, your instinct is likely to want to hurt back. Ever been in a situation in which you held the power to get even with someone? Maybe you did, maybe you didn't. Think about what you would have done in Joseph's situation.

> The depth of your hurt determines the width of your response.

Through a series of twists and turns, Joseph eventually revealed his true identity to his brothers. In a powerful moment, he chose to forgive them. His words to them are poignant: "You meant evil against me; but God meant it for good" (Genesis 50:20 NKJV).

Not only did Joseph heal himself internally, he also healed and saved his entire family.

You have to love like you've never been hurt.

David had a father who did not believe in him. The prophet Samuel had arrived at his house to anoint the next king of Israel, at God's direction; Samuel told David's father, Jesse, "Bring out all of your sons. One of them is going to be king." David's father paraded seven of them before Samuel. He didn't even bother adding David to the lineup.

It was as if Jesse was saying, "There's no need to bring David out. He's a loser. He's a failure. He'll never amount to anything." You might be familiar with these words. Maybe you have even heard them from a parent. Does the pain still linger? Does that brokenness affect your current relationships?

David could have taken issue with his father. He could have used the pain as fodder when he got hurt by others later—including his bitter wife Michal, who made fun of him, and his son Absalom, who plotted to kill him. That is a lot of hurt caused by people who are supposed to love you the most.

> When you love like you've never been hurt, God will use even the worst that's been done to you for His glory.

While David could have gotten mad or even, he didn't. The Bible tells us David was a man after God's own heart. He kept on loving like he'd never been hurt.

You have to love like you've never been hurt. You have to refuse to be bitter. You have to refuse to get angry. You have to refuse to get even. When you love in this way, God will raise you up and use even the worst that has been done to you for His glory.

Jesus was betrayed by one of His own disciples. He was abandoned by others. Roman soldiers beat Him. They nailed Him to a cross. They stabbed Him in His side. They put a crown of thorns on His head. They took that cross and dropped it into the ground with a thump. Jesus' body shook as the pain was released through it. And He lifted His voice and said, "Forgive them; for they know not what they do" (Luke 23:34 KJV).

Jesus loved like He'd never been hurt. He loves us like we've never hurt Him. He loves us like we've never failed. He loves us like we've never lied to Him. He loves us like we've never done what we said we'd never do again.

Christ's love was not cautious, it was extravagant.

In imitating Jesus, we can love the same way, even when we have been hurt.

## Choose to Love Others—Always

Somewhere in your city is a young man who just told his Christian family that he's gay. Somewhere a young woman admitted to her parents that she is an atheist. Somewhere a teenager just got in trouble with the law or unearthed to his loved ones his battle with drugs.

As a parent, what are we supposed to do in these situations? Punish our children? Stop talking to them? Turn them away? Give up on them?

This is what we are supposed to do: Love them like we've never been hurt. Eat with them. Call them. Email them. Reach out to them. Be there for them. Tell them, "I want to have a relationship with you because I love you."

When you love somebody, it will never fail. When you love somebody, that love will get to them.

Sometimes we think we are doing a good thing when we refuse to have any contact with loved ones who are not living up to our standard. This is not true. I will talk more about this in the next chapter, but know this: Love never fails.

God has called us to love like we've never been hurt.

## Choose to Press Forward

If you have been hurt by someone—if you have been betrayed, abused, abandoned, gossiped about, whatever—there comes a time when you have to pull yourself from the pain of that situation and say, "Enough is enough."

Staying bitter, reliving the memory or harboring the pain leads nowhere. It's counterproductive. You have to choose to stop the cycle. Let it go. Leave it behind. Paul encouraged us to "press on to reach the end of the race and receive the heavenly prize for which God, through Christ Jesus, is calling us" (Philippians 3:14).

It's time to let God heal you. It's time to let God restore you. It's time to let God do a mighty work.

*But, Pastor Jentezen, I can't. It hurts too much. It's too hard.*

I get it. I really do.

## Choose to Heal Your Wounds

John 10:10 tells us the enemy's purpose "is to steal and kill and destroy." The devil does not fight fair. And he will not give up until you are wounded to death.

You may be dealing with a major conflict in your family. You may struggle in your marriage. You may have lost a child to cancer. When your heart is broken to such a degree that it feels beyond repair, the wounds grow deeper. And while not all wounds are fatal, if they do not heal, they can kill you.

The dictionary defines a wound as "an injury to the body (as from violence, accident, or surgery) that typically involves laceration or breaking of a membrane (as the skin) and usually damage to underlying tissues." A wound is more than a surface cut. A wound goes so deep that it breaks through and penetrates the soul and the heart of a person.

You may know what it feels like to be wounded by divorce, by abandonment, by bankruptcy, by seeing your kids every other weekend or not at all or by an addiction raging in your family. We all have wounds that seem like they cannot be healed. But there is good news: It is never God's will for the wound to kill us.

Jesus was "pierced for our rebellion, crushed for our sins. He was beaten so we could be whole. He was whipped so we could be healed" (Isaiah 53:5). Jesus received deadly wounds at Calvary, but three days later He rose from the dead. And when His deadly wounds were healed, a Church was birthed and a world was changed.

I find many of us struggle with the temptation of wanting to hide our struggles. We've been through stuff, but we do not want anyone to know. Instead, we put on a façade. We fake a smile, say the right things and hide the baggage. We want those around us to think we have the perfect life, the perfect marriage, the perfect family. We would rather pretend we are so spiritual that we are immune to crisis.

I know what it's like to want to hide the bad stuff and ignore the realities of a family in conflict. But, hey, I would be a fool to say I have never had marriage or family problems.

God wants to heal you from your wounds, but first you have to let Him. And before you let Him, you have to admit to your brokenness.

Now, you do not have to tell all of Facebook or your Twitter followers every single detail of your struggle, but it is important to surrender

> **God wants to heal you from your wounds, but first you have to let Him.**

them first to God. Ask Him to transform you, to heal you, to release you from bitterness, anger, fear, depression or hopelessness.

Close your eyes and take a breath.

You will hear Jesus whisper, "Come to me, all of you who are weary and carry heavy burdens, and I will give you rest" (Matthew 11:28).

I am not saying it's going to be easy. It's a process, sometimes a long one. As Christians, we want the instantaneous. We are a microwave generation that craves solutions to problems in thirty seconds flat. News flash: While God certainly does perform instantaneous deliverance, that is the exception, not the norm.

So pray and keep praying. Believe and keep believing. Forgive and keep forgiving. Talk to a therapist if it would help. Work through a twelve-step program. Read books. Get wisdom from godly counsel. Do what it takes to heal the wound.

Oh, and here's the thing about wounds: They heal, but they leave something behind—scars.

When Jesus appeared to the disciples after the resurrection, He showed them His scars, twice. It seems He was intentional about pointing them out.

Scars are nothing to be ashamed of. They are a testimony of God's ability to heal deadly wounds.

Scars are reminders of how bad it was at one time and how through Christ you overcame.

Scars are proof that though the enemy tried as hard as he did to destroy you or your family, the weapons formed against you did not prosper (see Isaiah 54:17).

Scars say, *I made it.*

*I came out on the other side.*

*I am healed.*

*I am whole.*

Learning to love like you've never been hurt requires wanting to heal and taking steps to make that happen. I will talk through that process throughout this book.

> **Scars are a testimony of God's ability to heal deadly wounds.**

While it may take time, healing can come; what has been broken can be restored. I mentioned this passage in the introduction, but it's worth repeating. Take the following words to heart: "The moon will be as bright as the sun, and the sun will be seven times brighter— like the light of seven days in one! So it will be when the LORD begins to heal his people and cure the wounds he gave them" (Isaiah 30:26).

God promises you brighter days ahead.

## Choose to Keep Driving

The movie *Black Hawk Down* is based on the Battle of Mogadishu, the longest sustained firefight involving American troops since the Vietnam War. In a raid in October 1993, Special Forces operatives were tasked with seizing two high-ranking advisors to a ruthless warlord. The mission was a success. After capturing the two lieutenants, U.S. troops began their return to base. Then the unthinkable happened.

One of the warlord's henchmen launched a rocket-propelled grenade (RPG) and shot down a Black Hawk helicopter. Two soldiers were killed and five injured in the ensuing crash, one of whom later died. Then a second Black Hawk was shot down. Three crew members were killed and one was taken hostage.

The raid quickly turned into a rescue mission to secure and recover the crews of both helicopters. For hours, gunfire rained down on the streets. More and more U.S. soldiers were killed.

In one scene in the film, right after the second Black Hawk helicopter is shot down, Army Ranger Lt. Col. (today retired Col.) Danny R. McKnight, played by actor Tom Sizemore, is charged with trying to get a small convoy of Humvees back to base. As the soldiers drive through narrow and winding city streets, they are assaulted by heavy gunfire. At one point, Lt. Col. McKnight stops the convoy to take in the wounded and dead along the way. He approaches a vehicle that has just been hit with an RPG. He and other soldiers nearby carefully remove the dead driver. Then the lieutenant colonel turns to a nearby soldier who has blood dripping down his face.

"Get in that truck and drive," McKnight barks to the obviously wounded soldier.

"But I'm shot, Colonel," the young man protests.

"Everybody's shot! Let's go."

Friend, you are not the only person to have been lied to. You are not the only person to have been betrayed. You are not the only person to have been abandoned. You are not the only person to be left behind. And you are not the only one who is trying not to give up.

I don't say this to minimize your pain. I say this to encourage you to keep moving forward.

Sometimes the people we have loved the most can hurt us the most. But you still have to get in the truck and drive.

---

To love like we've never been hurt is not something we can do in our own strength. We need the grace of God to help us make that phone call or send that text. We need the grace of God to tell the wayward child we have not spoken to in months, "I want to eat with you. I want to spend time with you. I want to reconnect with you." We need the grace of God to get through a crisis in our marriage and be willing to try again.

> Sometimes the people we have loved the most can hurt us the most. But you still have to get in the truck and drive.

I am not promising you an easy road, but I promise God can empower you to love others the way you ought to. He will help you stop fighting and start talking. He will help you stop yelling and start reaching out. He will reconcile your relationships. He will make your family whole again.

God will begin, little by little, to release you from the past if you will reach for a new day.

It takes a lot of love and forgiveness to hold a family together. Love never fails. Keep on forgiving. Keep on loving. Keep on reaching. Keep on talking.

A fruitful life is not an accident; it is a result of right choices. Choose to love like you've never been hurt. If you choose to forgive, forgiveness can rewrite your future!

Love never fails.

## THE **BIG** IDEA

The ones whom you love the most can hurt you the most. Love them anyway.

# CHAPTER THREE

# IT IS NEVER WRONG TO LOVE

When my friend Mac's only child, Malcolm, was a senior in high school, he told his father he was gay. Mac felt as if an eighteen-wheeler had just blindsided him. He'd had no idea. He didn't know what to think. He didn't know what to say. At the time, Mac's mind raced. *How could I have not known? How could I have missed the signs?*

Tears streamed down Malcolm's face as he shared glimpses of a world Mac never knew existed for his son. Malcolm told his father that since he had been in the fifth grade, he had been bullied because of his sexual orientation. He was constantly beat up, called terrible names and even spit upon.

Mac could not believe what he was hearing. Every day Malcolm had walked through their front door with a beaming smile, as though all was well in his world. He always seemed happy and carefree. The reality of Malcolm's world for the previous seven years, however, was anything but.

The summer before Malcolm's confession, father and son attended Forward, an annual youth conference at our church. My friend remembers how after one service, Malcolm was touched by God in a powerful way. He lay on the floor during an altar call, broken and calling out to his heavenly Father. "Why did you make me this way?" he pleaded in tears. Mac was moved by his son's vulnerable spirit before God, but he did not know exactly what the words meant. Now they made sense.

After his son revealed that he was gay, Mac initially felt hurt, he admits. Then he felt angry. He blamed himself. "I felt like I didn't take the time to see the signs. If I had, though I know I would not have been able to change him, I could have at least been there for him. I would have been able to hold his hand and give support while he was walking through what had to be the roughest time of his life. Being rejected by your peers and schoolmates has to be unbearable, not just at his age but at any age."

Eventually, Mac learned the best thing he could do as a parent was to love his child.

Mac's biggest fear was the possibility of Malcolm hurting himself. Suicide is the second leading cause of death among young people ages 10 to 24.[1] For gays and lesbians, the rate of suicide attempts is more than 20 percent higher.[2]

"There is no way I wanted my son to ever resort to suicide," Mac told me. "I knew I couldn't push him away or push my beliefs on him. All I needed to do was to give my son to God, pray for him and love him. I don't condemn him for his lifestyle. It's not my place. I simply love him."

Mac has learned a lot about what it means to love someone who is living a life contrary to what he has been taught, contrary to what God says is right. Here is what this amazing man taught me.

First, love your child because he or she is yours. We're not called to judge people, not even our own kids. We are called to love them. If I can't say anything that won't result in an argument, I just say, "I love you." Malcolm and I are very busy, and while we don't talk every day, I make sure he knows I love him. There are times I don't know what to say to him when we do talk, so I just tell him I love him.

Second, find common ground. My son and I hold different political and social views, but we fight hard to find things we both have in common or enjoy doing.

Finally, make adjustments. This looks different for everyone. For me, I refuse to follow Malcolm on many of his social media platforms. The more I see what he is doing, the more I'm inclined to worry. At the same time, when I visit him in New York City, where he lives, I go along with whatever he has planned. I'm just grateful to be a part of his world.

Recently, Mac and his son took a ten-day pilgrimage to Israel that was sponsored by our church. One of the neat things we offer is the opportunity to be baptized in the Jordan River, the same place where Jesus was baptized. I will never forget seeing Mac and his son walk into that cold river. As hymns were sung, they locked arms, ready to be baptized as a team. It was a sign of a father saying, "I love my son." The decision was made that nothing is going to separate the love between father and son, not even religion.

Mac does not have a perfect relationship with his son, but he believes, in his words, that "love will make it work somehow." My friend and his wife pray daily for their son. They love him without condition. They are not ashamed of him. And they have put him into God's hands.

It is never wrong to love.

## Love—Don't Judge

What do we do when someone is not living the way he or she ought to live?

Let me be clear: Sin is sin. This is truth. It's not up for negotiation.

But here is another truth: God never commanded us to reject people because they are not living up to a certain spiritual standard. Sadly, this is what happens many times.

**God never commanded us to reject people because they are not living up to a certain spiritual standard.**

If those we love are doing something that is wrong, often our judgment kicks into overdrive. Disapproval quickly trumps love. We refuse to have anything to do with those people. We announce to them and to the world that the relationship is over. And we do this in the name of faith, thumping our Bibles with self-righteous intolerance.

Do you remember what Paul wrote about love in 1 Corinthians?

> If I could speak all the languages of earth and of angels, but didn't love others, I would only be a noisy gong or a clanging cymbal. If I had the gift of prophecy, and if I understood all of God's secret plans and possessed all knowledge, and if I had such faith that I could move mountains, but didn't love others, I would be nothing.
>
> 1 Corinthians 13:1–2

We could have all the spiritual gifts in the world, but without love, they would be meaningless. We could quote Bible verses about condemnation until our throats are hoarse, but without love, it is meaningless. We could tell a loved one that what she is doing is wrong, but without love, our words are meaningless.

You might be shaking your head right now. Maybe you are thinking, *But we need to separate ourselves from those who are willfully sinning.* Later in this chapter, I will talk about what love means in the context of setting meaningful rules and boundaries. For now, though, I want to focus on what love means when someone is not living the way he or she ought to be living.

Here's what I've learned. Love doesn't say:

"You made your bed, now lie in it."
"I didn't raise you to do that, so I'm done with you."
"You did what? You're such a screwup!"

Love says:

"I will never agree with your lifestyle, but I still love you."
"I will never aid or abet what you're doing, but you are still and will always be mine."
"There is nothing you can ever do that will make you not be mine, because I love you."

Love does not demand its own way. It never loses faith. It is always hopeful. It endures through every circumstance.
It is never wrong to love.
It is never out of order to love.
You do not compromise your faith when you love.
This is what it means to love like you've never been hurt.

## Loving Doesn't Mean Lowering Your Standards

We all have to wrestle with the ever-present struggle between not wanting to endorse someone's behavior or actions and loving that person through it. So how do you do it?

Imagine a parent who just found out her seventeen-year-old daughter is pregnant. The father is the teenager's boyfriend, a boyfriend the mother does not like because he has no job, or maybe because he is of a different race.

When the daughter tells her mom the news, the mother is hurt. Disappointed. Embarrassed. Maybe even outright ashamed. And she doesn't get it. After all, she raised her little girl with values and standards and Christian beliefs. The family went to church together every Sunday.

The girl knows better, but here she is, a teenager about to have a baby.

This daughter lacks the wisdom and experience to know how to raise a child well. She may not even know how to change a diaper or burp an infant. Her boyfriend probably doesn't, either. The mother throws her daughter a baby shower, but instead of celebrating, all she can think about is how her little girl broke her heart with her foolish decision, one that reaped an irrevocable consequence that cannot be swept under the rug.

Now picture the scene in the hospital when the baby is born. Is the mother in the delivery room, holding her daughter's hand? Or is she home, upset, offended by her daughter's sin or offended by the boyfriend she doesn't approve of?

What would be so wrong in saying, "I don't agree with what you did, but I'm here for you"? With saying, "I love you, and I want to help you"? Would this make the mother any less a Christian than never speaking to her daughter again?

It's never wrong to love.

Billy Graham is often quoted to have said, "It is the Holy Spirit's job to convict, God's job to judge and my job to love." How many of us switch roles whenever it is convenient or when we are feeling super holy?

Look, there is a time and place for telling the truth in love. Sometimes we must address issues that are not right. We need to admonish our children and those we are closest to when they are doing something that does not align with Scripture. But we must do it in a way that is sincere and grounded in love.

If a friend has stopped going to church and stopped attending his small group, and you find evidence he is having an affair, I do not expect you to sit in silence, ignoring the obvious. The book of Proverbs offers us great insight: "An open rebuke is better than hidden love!" (Proverbs 27:5).

And yet, I have often seen this "open rebuke" lead to judgment and, inevitably, shame. Instead of reaching out to the friend, we exit the picture. Instead of calling and saying, "Hey, man, I don't agree with what you're doing, but I love you. And I'm praying for you," we tend to cut ties and refuse to associate with that person.

Something is not right about this.

None of us do what we are supposed to do all of the time. We have all fallen short. We have all sinned. We miss the mark often.

There is a Prodigal in all of us. Think about this—what would your life look like if God did not respond to your weaknesses, your sins, your addictions or your failures with grace and love? What if He gave up on you? What if He closed the door to relationship? What if He said, "Enough is enough. I'm done!"?

Talk about a world without hope!

You may not have raised your child to lie, cheat, steal, be selfish, be greedy, drink, do drugs or have sex before marriage, but if they are doing it, what then? Does it demand you withhold love?

Short answer: no.

But this does not mean that whatever goes on under your roof is acceptable or even permissible.

Moses conveyed boundaries to the people of Israel. God set boundaries and said not to cross them, or it would cost their lives (see Exodus 19:10–13). As parents, you have to set boundaries that you know are safe for your family. You have to set boundaries for yourself.

> **What would your life look like if God did not respond to your weaknesses, your sins, your addictions or your failures with grace and love?**

I would like to offer five truths on what loving like you've never been hurt means in the context of setting boundaries in your family.

## Truth #1: Standards Are Important

It has been said that the first generation *generates*. The second generation *motivates*. The third generation *speculates*. And the fourth generation *dissipates*.

It is possible to lose something from generation to generation in the transference of faith.

Even if your parents or grandparents were devout Christians, you might find your children today are receiving a watered-down religion, a faith that lacks substance, unlike the faith of past generations.

There's a lot of talk on family values in the world today. But what does this really mean? How does it relate to love? How does it benefit the family?

The dictionary defines *values* as "a person's principles or standards of behavior; one's judgment of what is important in life." Values have to do with our attitudes and our beliefs—what is important to us. They reflect our character and our identity. Establishing and maintaining clear values helps us make good decisions and sets our priorities on the right things.

I like to define three kinds of values that can help govern not only your life but the lives of your children: personal values, traditional values and core values.

### 1. Personal values revolve around your personal relationship with God.

Personal values are commitments and choices you make that are not necessarily commanded by God but reap great benefits spiritually. Personal values are not necessarily black and white.

For example, I cannot tell people that if they drink a glass of wine, they are going to go to hell. But my family and I have been blessed because our parents, grandparents and great-grandparents put up a barrier and said, "These homes are going to stay alcohol-free." Now, generations later, a lot of my family and I are in the ministry. None of us has ever been in rehab. This barrier worked. Before you remove a fence, you better ask why it's there. Guardrails line curvy roads in the mountains for a reason.

I also fast most Saturdays. Some days I fast half the day, other times the entire day. You do not have to fast to be saved. Nor does it make you a superstar Christian. It is a discipline. I feel strongly that God has directed me to do this on a regular basis. I can suggest this discipline to others—and I do—but I cannot impose this conviction and make you do it.

Jesus said, "If any want to become my followers, let them deny themselves and take up their cross and follow me" (Matthew 16:24 NRSV). The words *disciple* and *discipline* have the same origin. They go hand in hand. Being a follower of Christ means being disciplined. If nothing in you ever sacrifices anything for God, something is wrong. When you have a relationship with Jesus Christ, it becomes a *personal* thing between you and God. And you set personal values and disciplines in place to deepen your relationship with Him.

This includes disciplines like going to church regularly, serving others in and outside of church, praying and reading the Bible every day and choosing to uphold your physical body as a temple of God by not smoking, abusing substances or eating an unhealthy diet.

### 2. Traditional values are personal values that have been passed down from one generation to the next.

Traditional values provide a framework for your family in doing the right thing. "The land you have given me is a pleasant land. What a wonderful inheritance!" (Psalm 16:6).

My parents abstained from alcohol and transferred this personal value to me, which I transferred to my own family. Though years have passed, this traditional value has remained unchanged. Now, some people can get legalistic about these principles. Growing up, I was never allowed to go to the movies. Couldn't even go bowling or to the county fair, either. Many traditional values are just silly, so don't get crazy with this.

Pray and read the Bible to get a foundation for what is right for you—and use common sense. What is most important is setting traditional values in your home. Get your priorities straight. You love your children by giving them a foundation in the right things.

Both personal and traditional values are safeguards that protect your core values.

### 3. Core values are uncompromising biblical standards.

Core values never change, not even if society or culture changes. Jesus said, "The sky and the earth won't last forever, but my words will" (Matthew 24:35 CEV).

Core values are more than personal convictions; they are rock solid. Take the Ten Commandments: Don't serve idols. Don't lie. Don't kill. Don't cheat on your spouse. (See Exodus 20.)

You must have barriers set up to keep the core of your family intact. This includes barriers around your marriage, around your walk with God, around your anointing and so on. If we do not watch it, we will just keep stepping over the barriers. Once you start stepping over them, it gets easier, and before you know it, you do not believe anything anymore.

Loving our children means setting standards. This does not mean they will always follow them. But it does mean that you set the example for what is acceptable and what is not.

One more thing: Practice what you preach. Be personally accountable to the values you put in place in your home. Model your expectations. If lying is not acceptable for your children, do not fib about their ages at the movies to get a lower-priced ticket or at dinner to save a few bucks. Consistency is key. It is not about being perfect. There are no perfect parents because no one is perfect.

Atmosphere, like temperature, can have a real effect on the home. According to Scripture, as a parent you help create the atmosphere in your home based on the values you have chosen as your foundation.

> **When was the last time you added something to your personal value list instead of subtracting something?**

What kind of values are you building your home on?

Let me ask you another challenging question: When was the last time you added something to your personal value list instead of subtracting something?

## Truth #2: You Need to Draw Lines

Loving our children, even when they break our hearts, does not mean we let them do everything they want to keep them happy. Our goal is not to be the "coolest" parent on the block or to be their best friend. Our goal is to protect them.

Every year, when spring break would roll around, our kids would ask to go away with their friends. My wife and I knew a few parents who would give their children a fistful of cash, dictating the amount they could spend on alcohol, and even supply them with condoms. Their reasoning was, "Kids are going to be kids. Whether we like it or not, they're going to drink and sleep around anyway, so we might as well set parameters around the drinking and equip them to have safe sex."

I don't get that logic.

Love means establishing rules, enforcing them and refusing to accept bad or sinful behavior. Cherise and I have been pretty strict with our kids. We have set rules and have disciplined our kids for breaking them. Not everyone liked or agreed with the lines we drew. Over the years, we saw a lot of eye rolling, running of mouths and complaining when we told our kids that doing this or that would not be tolerated in our home. But rules are rules.

Also, the rules that Cherise and I enforce apply to all our children; we do not set one standard for one child and another for the others. We have a responsibility to our family as a whole.

We read in 1 Corinthians 16:13, "Be on guard. Stand firm in the faith. Be courageous. Be strong." As parents, we must be watchful and pay attention.

> **As parents, we must be watchful and pay attention.**

In ancient times, many cities had a watchtower on a hill. Someone from the community was stationed inside at all times to observe the surrounding areas and warn of impending danger. This person was on the lookout for animals sneaking in and destroying their crops and for enemies coming to attack. If he spotted something suspicious, the lookout would sound a warning to the community. It was easy to sleep well at night knowing someone was always looking out for you and your family.

You might be enduring a trying situation at home. You may have an inkling that your son is doing something he knows he shouldn't. You may have a gut feeling that your daughter is engaged in harmful behavior. Maybe your son has already walked out on you or your daughter ran off with some bad-news guy. You may feel so overwhelmed and frustrated that you want to call it quits. It is tempting to buckle under pressure and turn a blind eye, withhold love or even sever ties under extreme situations. It is harder to be present, to get up in their business.

I want to encourage you not to give up. Be watchful. Get up in that tower. Pay attention to your family. Pay attention to what is going on in social media. Get involved in your kids' lives. Check their Facebook, Instagram and Snapchat accounts. Block certain websites from your computer. Find out who their friends are. Confirm their whereabouts.

Eli was a high priest and a judge in ancient Israel, and yet the Bible says his sons were wicked. Some translations call Eli's sons "worthless." Eli and his entire house were judged because he did not restrain them (see 1 Samuel 3:13 NKJV).

Can you imagine God calling your kids worthless? But this verse tells us why. Eli did not "restrain" them, which means he did not put forth any effort to resist even the wickedness of his sons. Wow!

Want to show restraint? Give your personal values, your traditional values and your core values a place in your home. You do not have to hole up your children in their bedrooms for the rest of their lives and forbid them to watch TV, go to the movies, hang out with friends or listen to music. Set guidelines.

Friend, don't give up. There is a way to build up and fight for your family. (I will get into more of this in chapters 10 and 11.) I hope this will encourage you: When conflict breaks out in your home, when your child is doing something he or she is not supposed to be doing, remind yourself of these tips to help you work through the process.

1. *Attack the problem, not the person.* You are all on the same team, so do not take out your frustrations on your loved ones.
2. *Get all the facts before you offer advice or solutions.* Think before you speak. Nothing is more damaging than jumping to conclusions.
3. *Look for positives.* No matter how bad things get, in every situation, you can always find something positive. Look for it.
4. *Never withhold your love, no matter how rough the going gets.* It is okay to tell your loved ones how you feel, but make sure they know you love them unconditionally. When people feel loved and supported, they can weather just about any crisis.
5. *Check your words.* Your words are like nitroglycerin. They can either blow up bridges or heal hearts. You will be amazed

at the results when you refrain from hurtful words. Speak words that build others up. If you do not know what to say, say nothing.

Though we had many challenging moments when our children were teenagers, a few years later—some took longer than others—every single one thanked us for not letting them go to that party or date that person or attend a certain spring break trip with their friends. Of course, at certain times when Cherise and I were enforcing these rules, it felt like we were in the middle of a battlefield. But in the end, it was worth it.

## Truth #3: Love without Stopping

Look, sometimes people can do stupid things. This includes our own teenagers and others we love. But yelling at people with words of harsh judgment will not win their hearts. The Bible teaches that "human anger does not produce the righteousness God desires" (James 1:20).

Don't speak to the fool in others; speak to the king in them.

When your children do not do what you want them to do, resist the urge to power on the attack button. This usually involves a lot of shouting and yelling. Sometimes, in a fit of rage or other volcanic emotion we think we cannot control, we call our children names. We criticize them. We demean them with accusations like, "You're good for nothing," and, "You should be ashamed of yourself."

If you speak to the fool in your child, the fool will stand up. If you speak to the king in your child, the king will stand up. The prophet Micah calls for such a king in Micah 4:9: "But why are you now screaming in terror? Have you no king to lead you? Have your wise people all died? Pain has gripped you like a woman in childbirth." The King James Version phrases part of the verse like this: "Is there no king in thee?"

I believe inside every one of us is a king. I liken this to our potential to be the people God created us to be through Christ Jesus. We may struggle. But there is a king within us. We may fail. But there is a king within us. We may not be who we can be. But there is a king within us. Often, it is not easy to see the king or the queen in our own home.

So what is going to produce righteousness? The Bible offers a solution: "Love without stopping" (1 Corinthians 16:14, MESSAGE).

Your children may break your heart. Love without stopping.

They may say they hate you and will never see or speak to you again. Love without stopping.

People we love may make terrible choices. Love without stopping.

You may not like or agree with what they are doing. Love without stopping.

> **If you speak to the fool in your child, the fool will stand up. If you speak to the king in your child, the king will stand up.**

## Truth #4: Sometimes You Need to Love from a Distance

You may be wondering how to love someone who is toxic. This person may suffer from a drug or alcohol addiction, may be verbally or physically abusive or may have violent tendencies.

You can love in your heart, willing and praying for the person's good—from a distance. Being a Christian does not mean being a punching bag, a doormat or a crash-test dummy. Yes, God calls us to make sacrifices, to turn the other cheek and to forgive every offense. But He does not call us to have deep and meaningful relationships with those who have hurt us deeply. In these instances, it may be necessary to create intentional space.

My wife's biological father was not around by choice until she was thirteen years old. An addict diagnosed with bipolar disorder, he was not the poster child of a healthy father figure. As an adult, Cherise reached out to him multiple times. He would drift in and drift back out in a cycle that continued for years. This man got saved after my wife and I got married, but even as a born-again believer, he could never seem to get off the endless roller coaster of addiction and mental health issues. During this time, Cherise still tried to connect with him. She would invite him over to the house, even help him out with whatever he needed. Though she introduced our two oldest kids to their grandfather, she did not want him doing to them what he had done to her.

Whenever he showed up, I could sense a coming argument between Cherise and me. Since I was the only other male figure in the house, I would get the brunt of her frustration at his inconsistencies and toxic behavior. Finally, the cycle of staying and leaving took a toll.

Cherise had forgiven him a long time before, but after a while, she realized for her own sanity and the sanity of our family that she needed to love him from a distance. Not because she was better than he was. Not because he acted like a deadbeat. Not because he was too far gone for Jesus to change him. Because the relationship was toxic to our family dynamic, Cherise had to set strong boundaries. This meant determining what was acceptable and what was not, when he could come by, how long he could stay and so on.

There are certain people you just cannot keep bringing around in your life. You cannot disown them if they are family, of course, but you can love them from a distance. The less you associate with some people, the more your life will improve.

Be kind and firm in creating that space. You do not have to be a jerk about it. Think of ways to connect without daily face time. Maybe this means committing to a weekly phone call or a text to check in. Maybe you can write letters. Maybe you agree to meet the person for dinner somewhere other than your home, and you set boundaries, e.g., asking them to leave if they show up loaded. You may make room for these loved ones in your heart, but it is equally important to put physical boundaries in place.

### Truth #5: We Can Learn to See through the Eyes of Jesus

When we choose to love even though we've been hurt, even though others have made mistakes, even though we feel someone does not deserve it, we begin to love how God loves. Without condition. Without expectation. No strings attached.

Choose to see people through the eyes of Jesus. Love others the way God loves you. Then you will find a love so wide, so high, so deep, so long, you will never be the same.

## THE **BIG** IDEA

Love people who have messed up.

# CHAPTER FOUR

# STOP KEEPING SCORE AND START LOSING COUNT

M y wife and I never planned on getting tattoos.

Some tattoos look fine on other people, but we've never really been tattoo folk. From time to time our daughters would mention them when they were growing up, and our rule was, "Once you turn eighteen, you can put whatever you want on your body." Not that we ever imagined any of our kids would actually get one.

A few weeks before I finished writing this book, two of them had an announcement to make when they called my wife for a video chat. You can imagine her surprise when they held up the sides of their forearms and showcased their brand-new (and thankfully tiny) tattoos that read "70 × 7."

Cherise's jaw dropped to the floor. "Those better be fake," she said, trying to keep her cool.

The girls laughed and said, "It's Daddy's fault! He's been teaching us to love like we've never been hurt."

Well, I can't say I *made* them get tattoos, but a few days before this big event I *was* delving into some principles of forgiveness with them.

The back story: Someone had done our two daughters wrong. They had forgiven the person and moved on. Sometime later, that same person hurt my daughters again. It was a little harder to forgive the same person for the same thing the second time. I shared with them what I am going to share with you in this chapter, how Jesus commanded us to forgive—always.

When the girls detailed their tattoo adventure with me, one of them—I cannot remember which—said, "I remembered God's mathematics of forgiveness and how Jesus told us to forgive seventy times seven. I realized I needed a daily reminder to keep forgiving. So we got tattoos to help us!"

Our girls posted their tattoo adventures on Instagram and received thousands of comments, some from folks who admitted they needed the same daily reminder, which warranted a trip to the tattoo parlor. And, well, I never thought I would ever say this, but Cherise and I are thinking of getting that same tattoo soon!

## Math Problems

One of the most powerful lessons Jesus ever taught was on forgiveness.

He gave it because Peter approached Jesus and asked, "Lord, how often should I forgive someone who sins against me? Seven times?"

"No, not seven times," Jesus replied, "but seventy times seven" (see Matthew 18:21–22).

I have a sneaky suspicion Peter had someone in mind that he had already forgiven six times. He just might have been ready to write that person off. Whether or not, he was looking for a formula.

I have struggled with math since I was a kid. I have never been good at it. Even today, if I am paying for a meal at a restaurant and I am tasked with figuring out the tip, whoever I am with had better go ahead and order dessert and coffee, because we're going to be there for a while.

Maybe you feel my pain. I do not know your skill set, but I do know that, no matter how bad we are at math, most of us are good at keeping score when it comes to people who have caused us harm.

Some of us even have photographic memories when it comes to holding a grudge. We know exactly the year, the month and the precise time of day of every single offense that has come our way. We create mental spreadsheets for each person who has hurt us and start tallying up marks for every offense.

"My spouse criticized the way I look." *Check.* "Then he (she) forgot my birthday." *Check.* "Then he (she) refused to have sex with me, blaming it on a headache I know he (she) didn't have." *Check.* "My co-worker took credit for my project." *Check.* "Then she took credit for my work." *Check.* "Then she made a snide remark about my job performance." *Check.* And on and on and on.

Many of us have trouble forgiving. Instead of releasing offenses, we cling to them for dear life. We turn them into mathematical absolutes. Some of us carry misconceptions about forgiveness that prevent us from forgiving. I hope to clear some of these up for you toward the end of this chapter and, if you need it, help guide you toward forgiveness.

No matter how many times we have been hurt, the Bible is clear on one thing: We must forgive.

Want to learn to love like you've never been hurt? Start forgiving.

When Peter blurted out "seven times," he thought he was being generous. You might think the number is on the low side. How many times does a friend get to stab you in the back before you are done with her? How many times does a parent get to criticize you before you never speak to him or her again? (Note, though, that not everyone you forgive and love needs to be a part of your life. I will talk about this toward the end of the chapter.)

Jesus had the perfect answer.

## Keeping Score versus Losing Count

Jesus says, "No, not seven times. Seventy times seven."

You know I am not good at math, but I *can* figure out this equation. The answer is 490. The way I read it, this means we are to forgive the same person 490 times each day. That is a lot of forgiving to do. At a rate of one act of forgiveness every three or so minutes, you could spend an entire day just forgiving someone!

But this is not about numbers. Jesus was giving us a new math formula, a new set of truths for us to walk in forgiveness. The first truth is this: Forgiveness is not about keeping score. It's about losing count.

We are all going to get hurt in some way. Your spouse will let you down. Someone might gossip about your marriage. Someone might steal your money. Someone might steal your husband. Someone may have abused you. Someone may have harmed your child.

**Forgiveness is not about keeping score. It's about losing count.**

While getting hurt is reality, getting and staying bitter is a reaction. We must live a lifestyle of constant forgiveness. This is not about satisfying the requirements of a mathematical equation. We must forgive. *All* the time.

## To Not Forgive Is Unforgivable

C. S. Lewis wrote, "Every one says forgiveness is a lovely idea until they have something to forgive."[1] Forgiveness is like money. We want to get it, not give it.

An unpardonable sin, found in Matthew 12:31–32, is the blasphemy against the Holy Spirit. For years I believed this was the one and only sin that could not be forgiven. But I was wrong.

Jesus also said, "For if you forgive men their trespasses, your heavenly Father will also forgive you. But if you do not forgive men their trespasses, neither will your Father forgive your trespasses" (Matthew 6:14 NKJV).

The second truth of forgiveness is that it is unforgivable not to forgive. If you refuse to forgive others, God will not forgive you.

Do you need God to forgive you for something? If you are human, of course you do. Well, then, forgive those who have wronged you, betrayed you, cursed you, abused you, harmed you, abandoned you, stolen from you or were unfaithful to you.

All of us carry debts we cannot pay.

After Jesus offered Peter the mathematical equation for forgiveness, He illustrated His point with a parable. "Therefore the kingdom of heaven is like a certain king who wanted to settle accounts with his servants" (Matthew 18:23 NKJV). You can read the entire story in Matthew 18, but here is my summary.

This king must have had a meeting with his CFO, or maybe he was a really smart man and did the accounting himself. As he scrolls through the financial records, he realizes a servant owes him ten thousand talents.

According to scholars, a talent at that time was the equivalent of a thousand dollars today. Therefore, this servant is in the hole for ten million dollars. I love what verse 25 says about this guy—"He couldn't pay." Well, that's obvious. No one I know has an extra ten million dollars lying around.

But the deeper meaning of this is that it is a direct reference to our sin debt. Jesus is our king. He knows we owe Him. He knows we have not paid up. He knows our outstanding debts.

So what does the king do? Does he send a team of tall and burly armed goons to find the guy, drag him to the palace and make him cough up the dough, or else? Well, that is sort of what happened, minus the scary-looking goons. When the servant shows up before the king, he throws himself on the ground and begs for mercy.

"I'm so sorry. Please show me some grace. I have a wife and kids! Give me some time, and I'll pay you back. I promise!"

The king is so moved with compassion, he agrees to forgive the debt and lets the guy go. Just as the highest authority in the kingdom forgave a servant, so Jesus, through the cross, forgives our debt.

The King of kings forgives all the vows we make and break. He forgives all the lying, cheating and stealing we do. He forgives our nasty attitudes. He forgives our gluttonous appetites. He forgives our idolatry. He forgives the stuff we look at on the computer. He forgives our addictions, our toxic behaviors, our gripes, our hatred, our biases, our prejudices.

Jesus forgives us. Period.

I imagine the servant leaves the palace on a high. I would have. His slate is wiped clean. He is no longer weighed down by a staggering financial burden. He can finally get a good night's sleep.

On his way home, the guy runs into a man who owes him money—a hundred denarii, to be exact. In modern times, this chum's debt would be the equivalent of ten to fifteen thousand dollars. You might expect the servant to pay forward the mercy he received an hour or so ago.

He doesn't.

The newly debt-free man rushes toward the other servant, puts his hands around his throat and starts choking him. "Pay me what you owe!" he yells.

It's like *déjà vu*. The fellow servant wriggles out of the death grip, crumbles to the ground like a rag doll and begs for forgiveness. "I'm so sorry. Please show me some grace. I have a wife and kids! Give me some time, and I'll pay you back. I promise!"

The first servant refuses even to give the guy a grace period, let alone forgive the debt. Instead, he has him thrown in prison. Other servants milling around watch the brutal exchange and are horrified. One translation describes them as "grieved." These eyewitnesses hurry off to tell the king what has happened.

> **If you do not release forgiveness, you will not receive forgiveness.**

The king is furious. He summons his goons and demands they hunt the servant down and drag him back to the palace. When the two are face-to-face, the king says, "You evil servant! I forgave you that tremendous debt because you pleaded with me. Shouldn't you have mercy on your fellow servant, just as I had mercy on you?"

The king is so enraged, he turns the guy over to palace torturers to do whatever they want until he can pay back every single penny of the original ten-million-dollar debt.

Jesus ended this powerful parable by saying, "That's what my heavenly Father will do to you if you refuse to forgive your brothers and sisters from your heart" (verse 35).

If you do not release forgiveness, you will not receive forgiveness.

## The Best Brought Out by the Worst

A third principle of forgiveness is that the best in us can only be brought out by the worst done to us.

We do not like what happened to us. It hurt. It broke our hearts. But the truth is that sometimes the best in you will never be released until the worst has been done to you. And usually it will be done by people whom you have loved, trusted and helped the most. God does not intend for the painful experiences in your life to destroy you.

Airplanes take off into a headwind because it gets them off the ground quickly. The resistance gives them lift. Opposition can do the same thing to you. Someone hurting you, betraying you or talking bad about you can bring something good. It can take you higher.

Right before God took Elijah up to heaven, He sent a whirl-wind. It came not to tear the prophet down but to take him up. The strong winds of adversity will lift you up, not destroy you. They will use the worst things done to you to bring out the best in you.

## Keep Tapping

Sometimes we think we have forgiven someone, but we haven't.

Here is a clue: If you still feel embittered when you hear that person's name or just cannot stop thinking about what happened, you have more work to do.

I know how hard it is to forgive. The pain is real. It sits. It festers. It builds. How on earth do we let it go?

The Heinz company used to sell ketchup in glass bottles. Today, you will only find them in restaurants; squeezable containers have taken over on the grocery shelves. They do not look as nice, but the plastic packaging makes it easy to get the ketchup out.

Wondering what ketchup has to do with forgiveness? Stay with me for a minute.

The glass bottles are a little tricky. You may remember having to turn the bottle over and pound the bottom of the glass with the palm of your hand. Often, barely any ketchup came out. Maybe you have tried to bang the side of the bottle on a table. Or, like me, you have tried to scrape the ketchup out with a knife. These tricks did not work well most of the time. (No wonder they invented squeeze bottles!)

I want to tell you a secret that, according to the Heinz company, very few consumers know[2]: The trick to getting the ketchup out of a glass bottle is to break the air bubble, a common byproduct of packaging foods under pressure. You have to tap on the glass where the 57 is, and keep tapping. Ketchup will begin to pour, though slowly. You have to wait; it is not going to plop out fast. It might take a minute.

This is how forgiveness works. You have to hit the right spot. Sometimes the contents of forgiveness are released slowly. This is especially true right after someone hurts you. But you have to keep tapping. You have to pray and keep praying. You have to forgive and keep forgiving. You have to love and keep loving.

I have pointed out that this generation wants things fast. Maybe it is not just a generational thing. Maybe it is the pressure of our culture. If we cannot get our food served or problems solved this instant, if we cannot get the perfect body or the perfect marriage by the end of the month, well, that's just not good enough.

Jesus said,

> Keep on asking, and you will receive what you ask for. Keep on seeking, and you will find. Keep on knocking, and the door will be opened to you. For everyone who asks, receives. Everyone who seeks, finds. And to everyone who knocks, the door will be opened.
>
> Matthew 7:7–8

If you are having trouble forgiving someone, be encouraged. You need to keep praying.

Keep asking.

Keep seeking.

Keep knocking.

And, little by little, tap by tap, God will help you release forgiveness. It may take time. But don't stop.

When we are on our knees, we are hitting the right spot. It is hard to hate someone you are praying for.

**Forgiveness will come if you do not give up.**

Forgiveness will come if you do not give up.

## The Struggle Is Real

As a pastor, I have presided over hundreds of funerals. One of them has always stood out among the others for a reason I am sure you could never imagine.

After I gave a brief message and sat down, the funeral director invited the family of the deceased to walk toward the front of the room. It was their chance to view their loved one's body in the open casket and say good-bye for the last time. This is always an emotional moment that sees many tears shed.

I sat toward the side of the room, minding my own business, when I noticed two women causing a stir by the casket. I recognized them as the daughters of the elderly woman who had died.

"Mama gave it to me!" one of them yelled at the other, while pointing to a ring on the finger of their dead mother.

"No!" the other screamed. "She gave it to me. The ring belongs to me!"

They yelled back and forth for a bit. Then one of them reached into the casket and grabbed the ring they were fighting about. Everyone who watched the spectacle, myself included, gasped. But the other woman was not about to let her sister take the ring that, in her mind, clearly belonged to her. She tried to jerk the ring off herself.

As the two grown sisters played tug-of-war with their dead momma's finger, I sat dumbfounded. I looked at the funeral director for some guidance. He didn't say a word. He just sat there with his mouth hanging open.

As I look back on it, in some ways it was pretty funny. And it makes for a good story. But the struggle was real. It was sickening to watch sisters get into a physical altercation right next to their dead mother lying in a casket. Sadly, this is a scene the enemy loves to sit back and watch unfold.

Bitterness will make you do crazy things, like pull on a dead woman's finger.

I have noticed that when people struggle with unforgiveness, it shows. This is an absolute: Hold on to a grievance or hate as if your life depended on it, and I will show you emotional, spiritual and even physical decay.

Research has consistently shown links between the mind and body. What we think about manifests physically. According to the Mayo Clinic, holding a grudge has a negative effect on the cardiovascular and nervous systems. One study has shown that people who thought about an offense regularly experienced high blood pressure, elevated heart rates and increased muscle tensions.[3]

On the contrary, here is what you get when you forgive: healthier relationships, greater spiritual and psychological well-being, less anxiety, lower blood pressure, fewer symptoms of depression, a stronger immune system and improved heart health.[4] Seems like a pretty good deal. And a no-brainer.

Releasing the emotional burden of unforgiveness can even result in a physical unburdening, as discovered by authors at Erasmus University, the National University of Singapore and the University of Maryland, who collaborated on a pair of studies. In the first, they asked participants to estimate the slope of a hill. Those induced to feel forgiveness perceived the hill to be less steep than the group induced to feel unforgiveness. The second study was more active. Participants were tested on a vertical leap. Those who forgave jumped higher than those who did not forgive.[5]

The weight of unforgiveness will drag you down. It is too heavy a load to carry in the race you are called to run. So stop keeping score. Start losing count.

Keep tapping.


## Release the Power

Forgiveness holds the key to freedom, to healing, to wholeness.

71

When Jesus was hanging on the cross before He died, He looked down at a wretched scene. The religious leaders were ridiculing Him. The Roman soldiers were casting lots for His clothes. The crowd was cursing Him with raised fists. And, as His body was stretched out on two pieces of splintered wood, He pleaded on behalf of the very people who were spitting at Him, plucking away the hairs of His beard, calling Him a good-for-nothing fraud.

Jesus asked His heavenly Father to "forgive them, for they don't know what they are doing" (Luke 23:34).

In one hour, forgiveness saved the world.

When Jesus uttered these words, His spirit was released. This happened right before He took his final breath and committed His spirit into His Father's hands (see Luke 23:46). Jesus' spirit could only be released in an atmosphere of forgiveness.

Before He could leave this earth, Jesus had to forgive those who were torturing Him, those who were mocking Him, those who were blaspheming Him. This was important because God's hands will not touch spirits that do not release forgiveness. Wherever you release forgiveness, you release the power of the Spirit of God.

> Wherever you release forgiveness, you release the power of the Spirit of God and the power of healing.

When Jesus released forgiveness and finally died on the cross, heaven and earth collided. The earth shook. The veil of the temple was torn in two. Rocks were split in half. Graves were torn open. (See Matthew 27:51–52.) As Paul wrote, "In this way, he disarmed the spiritual rulers and authorities. He shamed them publicly by his victory over them on the cross" (Colossians 2:15). When you forgive, you also release the power of victory over the devil.

There is more: When we forgive, we release God's power in our lives to bring healing.

The writer of the book of James asked,

Are any of you suffering hardships? You should pray. Are any of you happy? You should sing praises. Are any of you sick? You should call for the elders of the church to come and pray over you, anointing you with oil in the name of the Lord. Such a prayer offered in faith will heal the sick, and the Lord will make you well. And if you have committed any sins, you will be forgiven.

James 5:13–15

The first healing God ever did on this planet that is recorded in the Bible was not of a human being. It was of bitter water. In Exodus 15, we read how God led an estimated two million Israelites from the salty Red Sea to the waters of Marah, which means "bitter" in Hebrew. God did not heal a disease or a broken bone. He healed bitterness. He knew if He could get the forgiveness released and the bitterness out, the healing would come. When you forgive, you release the power of healing.

As Corrie ten Boom put it, "Forgiveness is the key that unlocks the door of resentment and the handcuffs of hatred. It is a power that breaks the chains of bitterness and the shackles of selfishness."[6]

This is coming from a woman who was imprisoned in a Nazi concentration camp for daring to help many Jews escape the Holocaust during World War II. She often witnessed prisoners, including her very own sister Betsie, receive brutal treatment from the prison guards. Betsie died while in captivity.

For years after her miraculous release, ten Boom spoke often in churches about her experience. One night after she had given a talk about the need to forgive, she saw among the crowd a Nazi guard she knew—one who had been in the same camp, who had been particularly cruel to her sister. He approached her and asked for forgiveness.

73

In her words,

> My blood seemed to freeze . . . I whose sins had every day to be forgiven—and could not. Betsie had died in that place—could he erase her slow terrible death simply for the asking? It could not have been many seconds that he stood there, hand held out, but to me it seemed hours as I wrestled with the most difficult thing I had ever had to do. And still I stood there with the coldness clutching my heart. But forgiveness is not an emotion—I knew that too. Forgiveness is an act of the will, and the will can function regardless of the temperature of the heart. . . .
>
> Mechanically, I thrust my hand into the one stretched out to me. And as I did, an incredible thing took place. The current started in my shoulder, raced down my arm, sprang into our joined hands. And then this healing warmth seemed to flood my whole being, bringing tears to my eyes. "I forgive you, brother!" I cried. "With all my heart!"[7]

The struggle is real, but so are the blessings.
Unforgiveness wounds. Forgiveness heals.

## What's Stopping You?

Years ago I counseled a woman whose husband left her and their four kids for another woman. I told her the first step to healing was to forgive him. My statement was not well received.

"But my husband doesn't deserve to be forgiven," she said, with tears in her eyes.

"I get that," I said. "I mean, he did a terrible thing that has caused you and your children great pain. He definitely doesn't *deserve* to be forgiven." I paused for a second. "But do you?"

See, none of us deserve to be forgiven. None of us deserve the grace that God freely gives. None of us deserve the mercies He renews for us every morning. None of us deserve to be loved with an unconditional, unfailing, unstoppable love.

I find that certain obstacles stand in the way of forgiving others. I know there are many and that everyone has a specific reason why the struggle is so hard, but I want to focus on these to clarify what forgiveness does *not* mean.

### 1. Forgiveness does not mean you forget what happened.

The old adage "Forgive and forget" is only a half-truth. Oh, and contrary to popular opinion, it is also not found in the Bible.

Forgive? Yes! Forget? Well, that is a bit tricky. When you forgive, you do not get amnesia. How do you forget the image of catching your spouse in the act of being unfaithful? How do you forget the time your uncle raped you? How do you forget the day your father abandoned you? How do you forget when your teenager wiped out your savings account to buy drugs?

When you forgive someone, you do not deny the offense. You do not pretend it never happened. It happened. It was real. It was bad. Forgiveness does not eliminate or minimize the severity of the offense.

But unforgiveness can cause even deeper pain. The weight of unforgiveness drags you down. It is too heavy a load to carry in the race you are called to run. Not forgiving others always leads to great bitterness, which will drain you of your peace and joy. By not forgiving, you sabotage your own well-being. When you forgive, however, you are released from the torment. You are free to love, free to have peace, free to be joyful, free to live a full life.

When you forgive, through the grace of God, you will begin to remember differently.

Instead of serving as a GPS coordinate for bitterness, the offense will eventually become a point of reference for how far you have come in the healing process and how much God has worked in your life to see beyond the hurt. Forgiving someone may be instantaneous, but the healing work takes time.

Take heart. Before you know it, one day you will wake up and that pain of being abandoned, betrayed or stabbed in the back will not be the first thing that you think of. And as each day passes, the hurt will lessen.

### 2. Forgiveness does not release the offender from consequences.

Sometimes we choose not to forgive because we think it means the people who hurt us will get away with what they did. We want them to own up. We want them to take responsibility for their actions. We may even want them to suffer like we did.

The number one reason why we do not want to forgive people is because we want vengeance. It comforts us. In Genesis 27:41, Esau said to himself, *I will kill Jacob after I have mourned for my father.* He desired to balance the scales of right and wrong.

Is it wrong to seek justice? I may forgive someone for killing a loved one, but it does not mean that person should not go to prison for the rest of his life. Likewise, the Bible does not teach that vengeance is wrong or sinful. In Revelation 6:9–10 we read about the souls of martyrs in heaven who stand under the throne of God, crying out, "Avenge us!" Sin does not exist in heaven, so these prayers must not be sinful.

Vengeance is not, however, ours to carry out.

The Bible says two things belong to God: the tithe and vengeance.

> Beloved, do not avenge yourselves, but rather give place to wrath; for it is written, "Vengeance is Mine, I will repay," says the Lord. Therefore "if your enemy is hungry, feed him; if he is thirsty, give him a drink; for in so doing you will heap coals of fire on his head." Do not be overcome by evil, but overcome evil with good.
>
> Romans 12:19–21 NKJV

It is not up to me or you to hold someone accountable who has wronged us. It is up to God.

Do not overcome evil with evil, but rather overcome evil with good (see Romans 12:21). Give God your anger. Give God your desire for vengeance. Allow God to be the judge and repay where repayment needs to take place.

God takes offense seriously. Jesus even said,

> It is impossible that no offenses should come, but woe to him through whom they do come! It would be better for him if a millstone were hung around his neck, and he were thrown into the sea, than that he should offend one of these little ones.
>
> Luke 17:1–2 NKJV

In other words, if someone offends one of God's own, it would be better for that person to have a cement block strung around his neck and be dropped into the ocean. Ouch! This is God's way of saying, "Vengeance is mine. Forgive—no matter what others do—and let Me handle the rest."

### 3. Forgiveness does not always mean reconciliation.

When you forgive someone, it does not automatically mean you must rebuild the relationship that has been broken. It might, but there are exceptions. Some people are untrustworthy or abusive, and to have close relationships with them would be unhealthy.

For instance, say you forgive someone who never apologizes and refuses to accept that he or she has wronged you. While forgiveness is still required, there is no way outside of a miracle of God that a relationship can be established.

If a parent sexually abused you as a child, you can forgive him or her without needing to become friends with your parent. If a business partner cheated his way through your company's profit margins, you can forgive him, but you do not have to go into business with him ever again. Reconciliation in any of these cases would be foolish, maybe even borderline masochistic.

Keep in mind that God has not destined you to be a crash test dummy. Simply forgiving someone does not invite more abuse by

**Let go so you can take hold.**

the offending party. There are situations in which you will need to set and secure boundaries.

I am not a licensed therapist, and I do not know your specific situation. But if you are struggling with knowing what healthy reconciliation looks like or if it is even warranted, I suggest you consult with a professional, whether a counselor or a pastor.

Stop making excuses for not needing to forgive. God is saying to you today, "Let go so you can take hold."

## Just Do It

Open your heart to forgiveness.

Do not wait to forgive until you "feel" like forgiving, because, frankly, it's probably not going to happen. Forgiveness is a choice, not a feeling. Rather than wait for warm and fuzzy feelings to wash over you before you think you can forgive someone, do it today. Depending on your circumstance, do it face-to-face, or if you cannot meet with that person, do it between you and God privately.

Sometimes those who have hurt you either have no idea what they did or refuse to own up to the transgression. Forgive anyway. Do not wait until the offending party has a come-to-Jesus meeting and begs for your forgiveness. This may very well not happen.

Forgive anyway.

Take the following practical steps to begin to walk in forgiveness today:

1. *Open your heart.* In order to forgive, you must open your heart. You cannot heal or move forward until you do this.
2. *Extend compassion.* In other words, try to walk a mile in their shoes. You do not know the story behind the person who hurt you. This is not easy to do, but try to separate the

person from the person's actions and have compassion on him or her. Again, this does not mean you excuse what he or she did or minimize the severity of the offense.

3. *Release the person from the prison you put them in inside your heart.* When you say, "I will never forgive so-and-so as long as I live," you have just put that person in prison in your heart. It is time to let the offender out. There is no doubt that he or she broke your heart, betrayed your trust or did something bad, but in order to heal and be whole, you must unlock the prison and let that person go.

Forgiveness is a decision. Choose to forgive.

As you read this chapter, I wonder if an image has repeatedly come to your mind, specifically the face of someone who has hurt you. This is God showing you whom you need to forgive.

I ask you today to join the 70 × 7 club. Do not forgive just once or even seven times. Commit to a lifestyle of forgiveness. This will change your life.

Whatever wrong has been done against you, you have obsessed over it long enough. Move on. One of the enemy's most successful strategies is to get you to focus on things that do not matter anymore. Why spend the only life you will ever have trying to justify the past when you can move forward into the blessing of God?

> **I ask you today to join the 70 × 7 club.**

Do not run away from forgiveness. Run to forgiveness. It is a great friend. If you choose to forgive, your heart will heal.

## THE BIG IDEA

Stop keeping score and start losing count.

# CHAPTER FIVE

# LOVE STARTS HERE

*We need to live life full throttle.*
*Live joyfully, live passionately, love completely.*
*Love completely now, because you're not promised another day.*

I stared at the notes from the sermon I was scheduled to preach the next day. The dark storm in our family that I shared in chapter 1 was raging. My message was a reminder of how short life is and that we need to stop harboring resentment, bitterness and anger. The longer I stared, the louder the whisper.

*Hypocrite.*

I thought of Paul's admonishment to church leaders in 1 Timothy. *Clean up your act at home before you start leading others in the Church.* Or, as I have heard it said, if it doesn't work at home, don't export it.

*Hypocrite.*

I was trying to keep things together in our family. I was trying to keep the peace while one of our daughters navigated through rocky waters. I was trying my best to love my family as Christ loves the Church.

I'll admit—there were times I struggled with feeling like a failure.

*Hypocrite.*

I wondered if perhaps I was shouldering the weight of too many responsibilities. Maybe the pressures of the church, the TV ministry, the building programs, the budgets and the constant traveling were all too much. I wondered if I should quit. Maybe it was best to hand in my resignation letter as a pastor and let someone else take over.

> **Shame does not have to lead you. Love can.**

A few hours later, I had a heart-to-heart with a close friend. We prayed. We talked. And I was reminded of the truth. I was not a hypocrite. I was human. I was a child of God. And I was loved.

The wounds of shame can run deep. And like muddied ruts, you can get stuck in them.

But I have good news for you. Shame does not have to lead you. Love can.

## Love Yourself First

This love must first be directed toward ourselves, because how we love ourselves affects how we love others. But don't take my word for it.

An expert in the law once asked Jesus which is the greatest commandment. Read carefully His answer: "'You must love the LORD your God with all your heart, all your soul, and all your mind.' This is the first and greatest commandment. A second is equally important: 'Love your neighbor as yourself'" (Matthew 22:37–39).

Jesus sums up hundreds upon hundreds of commandments, old and new, in one word: love. But there is a catch to the loving others part. We need to know how to love ourselves first.

I like to say that we need to feel good about ourselves, though not in a narcissistic, materialistic or selfish way. I am talking about an unshakeable inner confidence based on what God says about us, not a distorted self-image based on what the devil likes to throw in our faces.

Are you the one who had the affair? Or did your spouse cheat on you? Is your son struggling with a drug addiction? Do you feel like a failure because you cannot reconcile your family?

Messes have a way of diminishing our self-love capacity. And in this place, the devil thrives. He likes to whisper familiar phrases in our ears:

*You're not good enough.*

*You're not holy enough.*

*You're lazy.*

*You're undisciplined.*

*You call yourself a Christian, and you still can't get it together?*

When we judge ourselves unworthy, we miss out on the treasures God has in store for us. This reminds me of the time Paul and Barnabas were preaching to a crowd of practically an entire city. Some of the Jewish people, jealous of Paul, caused a scene, contradicting everything he was saying.

Paul was not intimidated; in fact, he grew bold. He responded to their shenanigans by declaring, "It was necessary that we first preach the word of God to you Jews. But since you have rejected it and *judged yourselves unworthy* of eternal life, we will offer it to the Gentiles" (Acts 13:46, emphasis mine).

The Jews were unable to receive from God. But not because of sin. And not because of God. And not because of Satan. *They* were the problem. These people were hindered from everlasting life because of their own self-judgment.

Love yourself and stay out of your own way. Sometimes your worst enemy is you.

I wonder how many blessings we miss out on because we feel we are unworthy. How many times have we opted out of God's goodness because we feel we do not deserve the manifestation of His glory?

Note, this is not about us. We are not worthy based on our own merit. We are worthy through Jesus Christ and Him alone. Once we start to recognize our worth in Him, things change. We begin to open ourselves to the great things God has in store for us.

## When We Cannot Love Ourselves

It is amazing how loudly the whispers of self-condemnation haunt us. Day after day. Night after night. For years on end, sometimes. It is no wonder we cannot fully grasp Jesus' mandate for us to love others.

When we let lies overrule love, it affects those around us. We tend to take out our frustrations, lack of self-worth, shame or guilt on those we love. We cannot possibly love like we've never been hurt if we do not love ourselves.

You may know exactly what I am talking about. If you struggle with depression, you may isolate yourself from others and, in the process, stunt the growth of healthy relationships. If you struggle with shame, you may have trouble extending grace to others. If you struggle with finding self-worth, you may find it difficult to trust those around you.

Jesus knew full well the problems that would come from a lack of self-love. That is why He did not respond to the scribe's question by blurting out a Tweet-worthy fortune cookie saying or a catchy sound bite.

Jesus *commanded* us to love ourselves. This was not a suggestion; it was an order. As we love ourselves, we become one step closer to the Kingdom of God, which is righteousness, peace and joy (see Romans 14:17).

## It's Not about How You See Yourself

Self-esteem is not the goal. God-esteem is. It's not about what you think about you, but what God thinks about you.

It does not matter what you have done or what has been done to you. Jesus sees you as a wonderful masterpiece. After all, you come from a bloodline of royalty.

I recently read an interesting article about horse breeding and a noteworthy stud named Tapit. Tapit is a white stallion at Gainesway Farm in Kentucky. Beautiful and elegant, he is a Grade 1 stakes winner; more importantly, though, he has sired an extraordinary number of offspring who are incredibly fast. His first crop produced a champion, Breeders' Cup Juvenile Fillies winner Stardom Bound. Many of his offspring have done remarkably well in a number of prestigious horse races.

**Self-esteem is not the goal. God-esteem is.**

Today, Tapit is the highest-earning stallion in the United States. The cost to breed him is $300,000 a pop. But he is not the most expensive horse in history. The late Storm Cat held a successful twenty-year career as a stud and at one point earned a breeding fee of $500,000.

Imagine spending half a million dollars (or close to it) to get a horse pregnant. When it is time for the mare to give birth, at first glance, what you get for your money seems a bit like a rip-off. Out comes a wet and sticky colt, trembling from the journey of birth. It stinks and is streaked with blood. On its knobby knees, the animal can barely stand.

But even though the baby horse is small and unsure, frail and mucky, the owners hover with pride. And they would tell you, with utmost confidence, that even though this colt had never run a race or had a jockey mount its back, every single dollar was worth it. Why? Because the horse comes from a line of winners. Its value is not based on its current accomplishments or awards. It is not

**You may not be where God wants you to be. But you are destined for the winner's circle.**

deemed worthy because of the many titles it has earned. It is living, breathing royalty.

Our bloodline is Jesus Christ. We have winner's blood pumping through our veins. You may have failed. You may have been sidelined. You may have been crushed by life. You may not be where God wants you to be. But you are destined for the winner's circle. You are an overcomer by the blood of the Lamb and the word of your testimony (see Revelation 12:11).

If you are not there yet, hold on. God wants to make you over.

### Get Ready for a New You

Do you remember the reality show *Extreme Makeover*? How about *The Swan*? In these two television series, ordinary men and women undergo plastic surgery, intense fitness regimes and even dental work to transform into something beautiful.

A tired housewife who let herself go while running after three young children spends a few weeks away from her family and returns all glammed up. A pot-bellied man who had more interest in working than working out goes away to makeover boot camp and comes back looking like Prince Charming. Today, the surgeons are taking over these kinds of reality TV shows. Series like *Botched* and *Dr. Miami* show the ins and outs—and befores and afters—of plastic surgery as patients go under the scalpel in hopes of feeling better about themselves.

Society places great emphasis on external looks. Every year, plastic surgery procedures increase in number. In 2016, 1.7 million surgical cosmetic procedures were performed. This does not include 17.1 million minimally invasive cosmetic procedures like Botox and laser hair removal. Before you start throwing some shade, this is a judgment-free zone. I am not shaming anyone who has had or is thinking of having cosmetic work done. I am sure we all have parts of our physical bodies we wish we could change.

I am writing about this because I believe it echoes our spiritual condition.

Sin and shame have a way of making us feel ugly. So do circumstances. You may feel empty or worthless because your marriage is shattering right before your eyes. You may feel hopeless because you just lost a child. You may feel like God's promises are not for you because your faithful prayers to break the chains of addiction seem to fall on deaf ears. If so, you need a boost. You need an extreme makeover. Luckily, we serve a God of the new.

God can give you a new look.

God can give you a new beginning.

God can give you a new life.

God can give you a new outlook.

Most if not all plastic surgeons maintain a portfolio showcasing their work on patients. You can flip through hundreds of photographs and see firsthand how much "better" the people looked after whatever procedure they had.

The Bible, too, is full of befores and afters. Jacob, once a swindler, transformed into a patriarch. The man possessed with two thousand demons traded a life of torment for freedom. The woman at the well realized her true identity in Christ, not in men.

Do you need a makeover? Are you holding on to excess baggage? Are you wearing past sins?

Think about your spiritual wardrobe for a minute. What do you wear that is outdated, ugly and ill-fitting? If you struggle with loving yourself as Jesus commanded, you probably own a lot of junky clothes. Like mom jeans. Or suspenders. (I'm speaking metaphorically, of course.)

You may not realize it, but some of you, as you look in the mirror each morning, rummage through your spiritual wardrobe and wonder what to wear, say this: *Let's see. What do we have here? Oh, yeah, I look good in this. I think I'll put my hurt on because I'm pretty comfortable in it. My dad hurt me. My husband hurt me. The Church hurt me. Yeah, that sounds good. I'll wear hurt.*

Or, *Hmmm, where is that— Oh, wait, there it is! I knew it was here somewhere. My past. I'm going to go about my day reliving the mistakes I've made. I'll just beat myself up thinking about every guy I ever slept with (or every drink I ever had, or every time I lost my temper).* Side note: One day of wearing the past is usually followed by a week of wearing guilt.

We wear all sorts of things that keep us in bondage. Shame. Condemnation. Brokenness. Fear. Anxiety. Anger. Unforgiveness.

Have you got a closet full of ugly clothes but have no idea what to wear? I'll make it easy for you. Jesus wants you to wear righteousness, peace and joy. He wants you to wear the Kingdom of God.

He wants to strip you of fear and clothe you with a sound mind.

He wants to take away your regret and give you renewing mercies.

He wants to throw out your broken heart and heal you.

He wants to remove your weakness, your problems, your mistakes, your regret and your past and shower you with grace.

TV networks need to put *these* kinds of makeovers on reality shows.

God can make over our families, too. He can take the old, dilapidated and broken parts of our homes and restore them. God can unite what has been torn apart. He wants desperately to do this.

But it starts with you.

Here's what you can do to start loving yourself:

1. Get out of the cage.

2. Renew your mind.

3. Put your shame on Jesus.

### 1. Get Out of the Cage

Years ago, I read a story about a bear that was captured as a cub and raised in a traveling circus. For years he was forced to live in a twelve-by-twelve-foot cage, drink dirty water and eat rotten food that had been pulled from the garbage.

Every day, on the hour, he would shuffle from one side of the cage to the other. Twelve feet forward. Twelve feet back. He would sway his big brown head back and forth while slowly taking each step. He did this every day for years, stopping only to eat or to sleep. It was quite a spectacle.

Curious onlookers would stop and stare. The crueler among the observers would throw cigarettes or rocks into the bear's cage, hoping to interrupt the animal's rhythm. But no matter what was thrown at the bear, he continued his twelve-foot shuffle.

Finally, the bear was sold to a local zoo. His new home consisted of sprawling green grass where he could play and sparkling pools in which to soak and bathe. He even had some fellow companions to frolic with.

When the bear arrived at the new place and zookeepers opened the door of his cage, they were shocked when the bear responded by doing . . . nothing. The bear did not move. The zookeepers had to force him out into the wide-open space.

When he was finally out of the cage, the bear stood up and took in his surroundings. He stood in the middle of an expanse. Freedom. Suddenly, the bear started once again his familiar, de-pressing cadence. Twelve steps forward and twelve steps back.

Zookeepers were baffled. They quickly realized the problem was not the cage but the bear's own mind. The bear was imprisoned by mental bars, not metal ones.

Some of you are dancing the twelve-foot shuffle.

The enemy has tried hard to permanently ink you with pain-ful memories, with failures from the past, with self-sabotaging thoughts, with fear of an uncertain future. He wants you to always see yourself as someone who has messed up. *This is who I am. I'll never change. I'll never get healed. I'll never become whole.*

When we are bombarded by the lies of the devil and begin to believe them, we become trapped in a small world. Instead of accepting freedom and running to Jesus, some of us try to find temporary relief by numbing ourselves with food, drugs, alcohol, sex or maxing out credit cards.

Proverbs 23:7 tells us that we are what we think. If we believe we are forgiven, redeemed, healed, whole and created for great things, we will become that reality. The truth of the flip side is tougher to swallow. If we think we are worthless, useless, good-for-nothing junk, well, so be it.

Therefore, we need to feed our minds with the good stuff. When you binge on negative thinking, replaying the hurt someone caused you or the hurt you caused someone else, it becomes a habit. That habit will then reap bad character. Once you establish bad character, it will affect your destiny. When you start believing the enemy's lies about who you are, you begin to destroy your destiny.

### 2. Renew Your Mind

So how do we turn off the channel of lies?

One way is to renew your mind. Romans 12 provides the starting point.

> Give your bodies to God because of all he has done for you. Let them be a living and holy sacrifice—the kind he will find acceptable. This is truly the way to worship him. Don't copy the behavior and customs of this world, but let God transform you into a new person by changing the way you think.
>
> Romans 12:1–2

It's about changing wrong thinking. It's about meditating on the Word of God and letting it penetrate deep into the core of our being. It's about recalibrating our minds by feeding on the truth. It's about finally getting rid of the bad tattoos in our minds.

Let's talk tattoo removal for a minute. While the process varies based on the size, color and age of the tattoo, generally speaking, it works this way: When focused directly on the tattoo, a laser (a high-intensity light beam) breaks up the pigment colors. After a series of sessions, the tattoo should be almost or completely removed.

What is interesting is that the laser needs some help in this process. Once the beams of light break the ink particles apart, white blood cells absorb these tiny bits and transport them to the liver, where, ultimately, they are excreted from the body. In other words, the tattoo is removed by light from the outside and blood on the inside.

What tattoos do you see in the mirror each morning that limit your potential? Or the plans and purpose God has for you? Or your ability to love yourself and others? Start beaming what God says on them like a laser. The writer of Psalm 119 says the Word of God is a lamp to his feet and a light to his path. The Bible is light to us, too, today.

When you read the Word, it works on the outside, pulsing the image the enemy has tried to permanently ink you with. It might be the image that you will never change, that your family will never reconcile or that your sin ruined everything.

As God's Word penetrates deep into your soul, the blood of Jesus Christ steps up from the inside with forgiveness and redemption.

Here's the deal: Legalism, going to church just for the sake of showing up or trying to be positive all the time does not cure low self-esteem, depression or negative thinking. They do not get rid of the mind games that plague some of us. Proverbs 16:6

says, "By mercy and truth iniquity is purged" (KJV). Mercy is the blood. Truth is the laser.

Get past your past by renewing your mind through the light and the blood. Here's how you can start: Change what you tell yourself.

Take a minute and think about your self-talk. Do you speak poorly about yourself? Talk back to your inner critic. The woman with the issue of blood in Mark 5 said within herself, *If I can touch the hem of Jesus' garment, I will be made whole.*

**Talk back to your inner critic.**

The most important battles we fight, many times, happen internally.

If you have a hard time loving yourself because of something you did, think about this: If God is willing to forgive you, you should be willing to forgive yourself. If you refuse to forgive yourself, you are holding yourself to a higher standard than God does. That is pride at an extreme!

The past can be healed in only one way: Forgive it. That is the one thing you can do for yourself that can change all of your tomorrows.

Before you continue reading the rest of this chapter, I challenge you to pray the following prayer:

*Father, I forgive and let go of all the mistakes and sins in my life. The lessons have been learned. I forgive everyone, and especially myself. Starting today, I choose to walk in love, and I thank You for the strength and grace to do it. Amen.*

### 3. Put Your Shame on Jesus

Finally, learning to love yourself means taking your shame and putting it on Jesus.

Most of us know the story of the Prodigal Son from Luke 15. A man has two sons. One demands his inheritance early and takes off to live in a city away from his family. There he indulges every sinful desire he has ever had. He parties. He drinks. He does drugs. He has a new girl in his bed every night.

When his money runs out, so does the fun, and so do his so-called friends. He finds himself broke, alone and very much missing home. Eating slop from a pig pen, the arrogant young man is now a broken one. He is tangled up in guilt and shame, kicking his behind for making such stupid decisions.

He wants to come home but cannot help but wonder what his father will say. Maybe he will shake his head and bark, "I told you so, you idiot!" Maybe he will not even open the front door. The son starts preparing an apology speech. Convinced his dad will not accept him back as a son, he plans to ask his father if he can remain in his household as a servant. The boy would get to live at home and have three home-cooked meals a day, and the father would get another worker to fix up the yard and take out the trash. It's a win-win.

Finally, the son wakes up one morning and begins the journey home. His stomach is churning from anxiety. His palms are sweaty. He is dirty and he stinks. And over and over along the way, he recites the "I'm sorry" speech he has been rehearsing all night long.

Here comes my favorite part. "And while he was still a long way off, his father saw him coming. Filled with love and compassion, he ran to his son, embraced him, and kissed him" (verse 20).

I find it interesting that the father ran to the son. See, in those days, the father in this story would have been the patriarch of his village. In this small, tight-knit community, everybody knew everybody, and everybody got up in each other's business. So when the boy left, it was breaking news. But he did not just break his family's heart; the young man also broke the law. And for that, he had to pay.

If a Jewish man left his community, went to live with the Gentiles, lost his wealth and returned home, the older men in the village would perform the traditional ceremony of *kezazah*.

*Kezazah* was a public display of shame. The older men would take a clay pot and throw it at the offender's feet. This symbolic tradition officially cut the offender off from his family, his community and his faith. After breaking the vessel into smithereens, the elders would shame the man with words. "As far as we are concerned, your ties with this community are severed. You have no place here. You have no rights here. You have brought shame to this village. You have broken your father's heart. You have broken the law of God. And we warn you that if you come into this village, we will stone you to death."

Ouch.

You can see why it was a good thing that the father saw his son from far off. He knew *kezazah* was coming. He knew the moment the elders of the community caught a glimpse of the Prodigal Son outside the village gates, the members of the judgment board would immediately initiate the ceremony of shame.

So with a fierce love that had not given up, the father rushed toward his boy. As he sprinted forward, the old man gathered up the hem of his tunic, consequently exposing his bare legs. It was considered shameful in that part of the world for a patriarch, a man of good standing, to run; not only that, it was also shameful to show one's bare legs. Double shame. But the father did not care. He wanted to get to his boy before the others did.

When the two met, it was like a scene out of a Hollywood movie.

"I'm sorry," the young man cried, throwing himself at his father's feet. "I'm not worthy."

"Oh, son," the father sobbed. "I'm just glad you're home." And, as tears flowed, he called his servants and asked them to bring the best robe and the most treasured ring, to put shoes on his feet, and to throw a huge party because his son was home.

The son could not have made it back home without the father. We cannot make it back home without the Father, either. We cannot make it back to God on our own merit, in our own righteousness. You don't get good to get God. You get God to get good.

A lot of people try to get home without the Father. Religion points to your sin, wags its finger and says, "Shame on you." Jesus welcomes you with open arms and says, "No, shame on Me." He takes your guilt and your shame and puts it on Himself.

> Religion points to your sin, wags its finger and says, "Shame on you." Jesus welcomes you with open arms and says, "No, shame on Me."

In 2 Corinthians 5:21, Paul wrote, "For God made Christ, who never sinned, to be the offering for our sin, so that we could be made right with God through Christ."

Religion will tell you God can never use you. Religion will tell you there is no hope for your family. Religion will tell you to carry the grudge. Religion will make you wear the shame. Religion will tell you to give up all hope of reconciliation.

Religion will tell you it is impossible to love like you've never been hurt.

God, however, will give you the grace you need and empower you to love like you've never been hurt.

God wants to restore you. He wants to offer you the ring of acceptance. He wants to reconcile you to the Kingdom. He wants to invite you to sit at His table. As it is written in Isaiah 61:7, "Instead of shame . . . you will enjoy a double share of honor."

Once we get ahold of the truth of grace, not only does it empower us to forgive and love ourselves, it should also prompt us to forgive and love others. Because, let's be honest, there's a Prodigal in all of us. And sometimes it takes learning to love through a mess to get to the miracle.

Now that you have read the Prodigal Son story in the Bible, let's put it in modern times. You may relate to the following scenario.

Lisa was raised in the Church. Her parents were great people who loved Lisa and wanted only the best for their daughter. She made the mistake of her life when she began to date Bill. After several months, Lisa was head over heels in love and wanted to marry him.

Lisa knew he had a drinking problem. He also had lots of excuses. She knew he did not like to go to church with her much, but she convinced herself that she could change him. Despite her pastor's warnings and her parents' pleadings, she went ahead and married him. About a year and a half later, she was in a living hell.

Bill's drinking evolved into physical abuse, and Lisa filed for divorce. She was heartbroken. She had ignored all the warning signs. Any time children of God marry children of the devil, they are going to have trouble with their father-in-law.

**"Instead of shame, you will enjoy a double share of honor."**

The good news is, God never gives up on us. Recovering from bad choices you have made can be a heart-wrenching experience, but God is always ready to restore you, to give you a new start. He said in Jeremiah 31:3–4 (NIV), "I have loved you with an everlasting love; I have drawn you with loving-kindness. I will build you up again."

## THE BIG IDEA

Learning to love others begins by learning to love yourself.

# CHAPTER SIX

# LOVING-KINDNESS

T hey want us to do a reality TV show," Cherise blurted out.
"Excuse me?" I did not have a good feeling about this.
"What about?"

"Our family!"

With these words, my wife burst out laughing. So did I.

A producer from Bravo, the television network known for its reality TV shows, had contacted Cherise. This woman had pitched to my wife her "brilliant" idea for a reality show about preachers' families. She was offering the Franklins a starring role.

For the record, I did not think the idea was brilliant. But Cherise has a relatively easy time convincing me to do certain things, and I agreed to take one call about the project. Mainly to get some information, and to use the face-to-face occasion to say, you know, "Thanks, but no thanks."

Right before the video call, Cherise and I could not stop cracking up about how absurd it would be to film "behind the scenes" at the Franklin home. So absurd, I admit, I would probably watch it. What was happening with our evening family devotion time would make for good TV.

Let me say this up front: I take seriously my spiritual responsibility in leading our family. I have always prayed for God to root our family in love and unity. But I will also be the first to say that there were times I probably went overboard in fulfilling my spiritual responsibility.

At the time, I felt led in my heart to gather the kids before bed and give them a three-minute message about a certain Scripture in addition to spending another three minutes in corporate prayer. I mean, in theory this is a great discipline. And God can work wonders when we make that commitment. Because it happened during the dark season in our family, however, trying to get everyone together in one place to pray, even for five minutes, was brutal. All the kids were mad at something or someone. And no one bothered to hide it.

Every night I would stand at the bottom of the staircase and shout toward the line of closed bedroom doors on the second floor. "Okay now! Everyone come down to the kitchen for devotions!"

Silence.

A few minutes would pass. Nobody would come. I would repeat myself, this time louder. Still nothing.

Cherise would finally get so fed up, she'd stomp over and yell, "For heaven's sake! If y'all don't come downstairs for devotions this instant, God help me, I'm going to come up and drag you down myself!"

And one by one our kids would schlep down the stairs, in slow motion, groaning each step of the way. By the time everyone had shuffled into the kitchen, three out of five faces were etched with stony coldness. It was clear most of our kids did not want to be there. But I did not care. I was going to lead this family in and toward love.

I would begin with an encouraging word. Then I would ask each one of our children to lead in prayer.

"Go ahead," I'd prod my oldest daughter. She would look down at the floor without saying a word. A few seconds would pass. Silence. "All right, then," I'd say and proceed to pray myself.

I'd turn to my second oldest. "Okay, it's your turn." My daughter would dart her eyes away from me, her arms folded tightly into her chest. Silence. I'd sigh and say, "All right, then."

It was like this with almost every one of our kids, almost every night, for a few months. Definitely not a scene you would want the cameras rolling for.

Back to the call.

Cherise and I listened as the producer suggested different angles for the show. The more I heard, the more I felt the need to shut the whole thing down.

"How many families would be on the show?" Cherise asked the producer.

"Three, but we can't tell you who they are."

Confession time. I am not the most computer-literate pastor on the planet. Though obviously we could see the woman on the other end of the line during the video call, for some reason I thought she could only hear us, not see us.

So, without making any attempt to be discreet, I elbowed Cherise to grab her attention. Then I drew my hand across my neck, you know, the universal sign for death. In other words, "Kill this conversation *now*." I also added some major head shaking to enforce my "No way!" sentiment.

The producer, of course, immediately noticed my dramatic body gestures. "I understand your hesitation, Mr. Franklin. But let me just say . . ."

She needn't have bothered. I simply could not imagine cameras in my house showing everything our family had going on. And, well, the rest of that conversation is not important. Cherise and I said we were grateful for the opportunity, but we weren't interested.

Even though we had a good laugh later, it did not diminish the struggle at home, which was very real. You might relate.

Ephesians 4:32 tells us to "be kind to each other, tenderhearted, forgiving one another, just as God through Christ has forgiven you." At that point, our family was not getting high marks for our acts of kindness.

### Kindness Takes Work!

When I was a bachelor, I never had a problem being kind to others. I was sweet. Patient. Kind. The poster child for Paul's chapter on love.

It all changed when I got married. I didn't turn into a monster or anything. It's just that married life was very different from single life. I was not on my own anymore.

No longer was I seeing Cherise just a few times a week—now I lived with her! I was doing life with her. Which meant I could not hide my true feelings. If I was in a foul mood, Cherise knew. If I was being impatient, she knew. If I was frustrated, she knew. And sometimes my attitude problem rubbed off on her.

As if that were not enough, then kids started coming along. Five of them. Tiring toddler issues morphed into complicated teenage ones. Let's just say I have learned many lessons about kindness along the way.

One of the most important ones is that it is better to be reconciled than to be right.

> **It is better to be reconciled than to be right.**

Do you know how many times I slept in the guest bedroom because I was mad at Cherise for something, usually something dumb? Funny thing is, she could not have cared less. She was the one getting a good night's rest in the comfortable bed all by herself!

Back in the day, heated arguments would occasionally turn ugly, peppered with unkind words and unfair accusations. Cherise would pull out her surefire weapon—and also her favorite statement—and hurl it in my face. "Ha! And you call yourself a preacher!"

I would then reach into my bag of mean verbal quips and pull out my favorite line. "You make me want to call myself a drunk!"

In many of the arguments we had early in our marriage, I would fight to the death to prove my point. I wanted her to see that I was right. But even if I "won," I paid a price for it. All it did was push her away and drive us further apart. It would have been better for me to shut up, stop trying to beat a dead horse and, instead, reach out to reconcile. We certainly do not talk like that anymore. If we did, I would not be writing this chapter.

It is not easy to be kind when the pressure is on. It is not easy to be kind when you and your spouse have conflicting ideas of parenting. It is not easy to be kind when your kids are out of control, when finances are tight, when your mother-in-law moves in or when you are the only Christian in the house.

But even through these things, we are called to be kind.

## Another Math Problem

If you remember, in chapter 4 I talked about how forgiveness is not a mathematical equation. We are commanded to forgive—everyone, all the time.

In the book of Ephesians, we find a formula that relates to forgiveness. Paul writes, "Get rid of all bitterness, rage, anger, harsh words, and slander, as well as all types of evil behavior. Instead, be kind to each other, tenderhearted, forgiving one another, just as God through Christ has forgiven you" (Ephesians 4:31–32).

In the first part of this Scripture, Paul tells us what not to do: Do not be bitter, angry and so on. In other words, drain the swamp. Get that mean and evil behavior out. Let it go. Put it away.

In the second part, Paul tells us what *to* do: Be kind, tender-hearted, forgiving. This is a test that lets you know whether you have forgiven someone or not. If you cannot be kind or tender-hearted, you need to keep tapping at your forgiveness issue.

> **If you cannot be kind or tenderhearted, you need to keep tapping at your forgiveness issue.**

But being kind is not just a byproduct of forgiveness. It is what we as Christians are called to do. It is how we love others as Christ loves us.

If you want to love like you've never been hurt, get rid of bitterness and start being kind.

Being kind means treating the waitress who serves you with respect. It means apologizing sincerely (and biting your tongue) when your neighbor cusses you out because your dog urinated in his yard again. It means you stop criticizing and putting down others, with your mouth or your keyboard, because they share a different worldview or opinion.

Now, I am sure you are not a mean Christian. You probably always smile and say please and thank you. But humor me for a minute; do some self-inventory. How would strangers and your loved ones rate your attitude?

Would you get a high score for being generous, for always lending a helpful hand, for being sweet to the grocery store cashier with the gauged earlobes? Would you be pegged as a poor tipper or a perpetually unsatisfied patron at your local diner? Would the members of the PTA board say all you do is complain? Would your spouse say he or she never knows what kind of mood you will be in when you wake up or get home from work? Would your child say you are always on the phone with your friends, running your mouth about what this one was wearing or how that one is a terrible parent?

You might be the kindest person in the world—if so, great!—but just maybe you could stand to fine-tune your kindness skills.

If you want to love like you've never been hurt, it is time to start being a kind person. All the time. Not just when the preacher is around, when someone important is watching, when certain guests are over for dinner or only when you feel like it. (Or when the cameras are rolling!)

Be kind . . . all the time.

When you are tenderhearted, you will feel moved by the haggard-looking single mom with the three loud kids sitting next to you at the fast-food place. You will watch her cradling a baby with one arm and with the other lunging for a toddler who is trying to put his boogers on your table. You will notice the third child throwing a tantrum because he wanted chicken nuggets instead of the cheeseburger. But you will not roll your eyes or shoot her dirty looks. You will get up, say something encouraging to her and offer to pay for her meal.

## To Be Kind Is to Be Holy

It is a shame when believers tout the right doctrine but have the wrong spirit. To be kind is to be holy. Want to know how holy you are? Determine how kind you are.

Paul wrote to the churches of Galatia, "For the whole law can be summed up in this one command: 'Love your neighbor as yourself.' But if you are always biting and devouring one another, watch out! Beware of destroying one another" (Galatians 5:14–15).

> **Want to know how holy you are? Determine how kind you are.**

The only reason we have or strive to have the fruits of the Spirit in Galatians 5:22–23—love, joy, peace, long-suffering, kindness, goodness, faithfulness, gentleness and self-control—is so someone can take a bite out of them and see what we're really made of.

Neither the world nor our families need more nagging, criticizing, whining and finger pointing. We are not going to make a difference in the lives of others by being petty, by yelling our opinions or by banging people over the head with our picket signs.

The world needs our open arms. The world needs grace. The world needs love. The world needs more kindness.

Through the years, I have received a few emails complaining about something or other in our church. *The music is too loud. The lights are too distracting.*

You know what? I have never gotten one single email complaining about how kind our church is. *No one* has ever griped that we are just too nice. Or that we smile too much. Or that we are too genuine. Or that we are too friendly. Funny, those are things that I happen to know people love about our church. We know how to be kind!

The law of kindness supersedes everything.

I know some churches are militant about where to let people park or sit. I understand that order is necessary, and in our church we try to maintain it as much as possible. But guess what? If a guest does not want to park where we tell him to park, we are not going to get bent out of shape about it.

We would rather be kind.

If a family does not want to fill up the second row of the church when the second row is empty and we need the space filled, we are not going to get infuriated.

We would rather be kind.

Recently my wife reminded me of a funny story about something that happened to her mother, Pat. Pat works for our ministry in Partner Relations, serving people who partner with us in our ministry. She connects with them sometimes by hosting them in our hospitality suite after church. Pat also loves to meet and talk to the people who come up for prayer during our altar calls.

A few years ago we were having a women's conference, and after an altar call my mother-in-law introduced herself and struck up a conversation with two women who had just finished praying. After a few minutes of small talk, they mentioned they were partners. Well, Pat just about died from embarrassment.

"Oh, my word," she said. "I'd love to invite you to our hospitality suite. Would you mind coming with me?" The two women looked surprised but followed her into the lounge area, where they sat down on a couch and helped themselves to freshly brewed coffee.

Cherise happened to walk into the room soon after. Her mother grabbed her by the arm and, with a wide smile, pointed her in the direction of the two women. "Honey, I'd love for you to meet two of our partners!" After my wife said hello and chatted with them a bit, she quickly realized her mother was mistaken. These women were not ministry partners.

Cherise nudged her mother to a corner of the room. "Can I talk to you for a second?"

"Of course!"

Once out of earshot, Cherise whispered, "Mom, they're partners. You know"—she paused and drew out the next word for emphasis—"*partners*."

Pat looked confused.

Cherise tried again. "They're not ministry partners, Mom. They're *life* partners. You know, lesbians!"

When my wife told me the story after it happened, I laughed, but I also felt challenged. It reminded me how important it is to show kindness to everyone in our church. Everyone.

We should not show preferential treatment only to people with whom we share the same theology or convictions. Our kindness should extend beyond who or what we are comfortable with. Why shouldn't we invite these precious women to the hospitality suite and show them kindness? What is so wrong or strange about that? The call to kindness has no boundaries. It is limitless.

> **The call to kindness has no boundaries. It is limitless.**

## Show Unusual Kindness

"It's not a good idea," the prisoner said with conviction. He pleaded with the Roman official and the ship's crew not to set off on the journey, but his advice fell on deaf ears.

The Roman official turned to the captain of the ship. "What do you think?"

Thumbing his nose at the prisoner, the captain answered, "Sir, this guy doesn't know what he's talking about. I'm the one with the experience, aren't I? Trust me. I've done this before, and I know what I'm doing. We're going."

"I'm telling you," the prisoner piped up, "we should stay where we are until the weather clears. If you proceed, much harm will come to this ship and to everyone on it."

"What do you know, anyway?" the captain hissed. "You're not a seaman, you're just a preacher!"

And so the ship sailed off to Rome with a transport of prisoners, including the apostle Paul, who had tried his best to convince the crew not to go.

As predicated, not long after the ship left port, all hell broke loose. A disastrous weather phenomenon, some form of typhoon, swept through the sea. Heavy rain pounded down. Visibility was zero. Violent gusts tossed the ship like a rag doll through towering waves.

The storm hammered these men for fourteen days straight. Every single one of the 276 passengers, including Paul, was exhausted and freezing from the constant battering of water and wind. Some of them had given up hope. On the fifteenth day, the storm still raging, the ship hit a sandbar. Under a barrage of waves, the vessel began to break apart. All the people on board had to swim for their lives.

Miraculously, everyone survived. Pummeled by Mother Nature, the men washed up on the shore of an island called Malta.

Half-naked and drenched from the continuous rain, the men threw themselves onto the wet sand, vomiting saltwater. Some still bowed over the pieces of ship they had clung to for safety.

As people kissed the ground in thanks for being alive and others sat in shock over what had happened, help came to them in the form of some wonderful people. The Bible tells us the natives of Malta demonstrated "unusual kindness" to the shipwrecked men (Acts 28:2 NKJV). The Message puts it this way: "The natives went out of their way to be friendly to us. The day was rainy and cold and we were already soaked to the bone, but they built a huge bonfire and gathered us around it."

The people of Malta were extraordinarily kind to these foreigners. They did not allow language, culture or race barriers to keep them from showing not just kindness but "unusual" kindness. They went above and beyond for total strangers. This is how we need to be to the lost and the broken who are washing up on our shores.

Do you show unusual kindness to those who are different? I am thinking of the neighbor who just moved in from the Middle East, the newcomer at church whose skin color is lighter or darker than yours, the store clerk with the foreign accent. If they washed up on your shores, what would you do? Would you ignore them? Would you allow your fears of the unfamiliar to supersede the mandate to love?

Now picture yourself aboard that ship.

You have been whipped by waves, battered by rain and wind. You feel as if you can barely hang on. And just when it looks as if all hope is gone, you wash up on some strange island surrounded by strange-looking people. And instead of kicking you back into the water because you are not from their part of the world, they welcome you with open arms. They offer you a warm place. They wrap a blanket around your shivering shoulders. They give you something hot to eat. They make you feel comfortable, right at home.

I call this the value of a warm place. We Christians should strive to be warm places for those who feel lost or have been pummeled by life.

For the person struggling with addiction and wanting to get help.

For the person beat up by depression and anxiety.

For the person confused about his or her identity.

For the men and women whose theology does not align with ours.

For those of a different race.

For the young people who are hurt because of mean, ugly, judgmental attitudes among some Christians.

We need to acknowledge the pain of others and warm them with the fire of the Holy Spirit. We need to tell them that God loves them and He has not given up on them.

> **We Christians should strive to be warm places for those who feel lost or have been pummeled by life.**

Some of you have experienced unusual kindness when you were stuck at a low point in your life. Maybe someone lent you a car when yours broke down. Maybe someone offered to watch your kids for free when you could not afford a babysitter. Maybe someone gave you a chance and invited you into a recovery group. Maybe, even after you made some terrible, life-changing mistakes, someone believed in you enough to pray for and mentor you.

Remember those blessings and share that same unusual kindness to others. Take the warmth and give the warmth.

## See the Treasure in the Field

The Bible tells us the Kingdom of heaven "is like a treasure that a man discovered hidden in a field. In his excitement, he hid it again and sold everything he owned to get enough money to buy the field" (Matthew 13:44).

If you are going to survive life and enjoy successful relationships, you are going to have to realize that everyone has a treasure and everyone has a field.

Often, we only see treasure when we are sailing smoothly, free of conflict and turmoil.

But when life happens and reality spills over into our relationships, we start to see the fields, warts and all. And then our attitudes begin to shift. We begin to criticize. We nag. We complain. Often, we feel we are entitled to do these things because the stresses of life are too much for us.

We are not called to be kind only when we experience the blessings of our relationships.

God has called us to buy the field.

In other words, when life gets tough and the one you love is not in a great place, you need to dig through the rubbish, the broken bottles, the piles of dirt, the manure, the rats and the beat-up, rusty cars that don't work, because buried in that messy field is a treasure.

You cannot have the treasure unless you buy the whole field.

You find the treasure in relationships when you choose to be kind. When you choose to believe in what is possible, not in your current reality. When you choose to reconcile instead of fight to be right. When you choose not to snap at your husband for no reason. When you choose to stop what you are doing and love on your **You cannot have the treasure unless you buy the whole field.** kids even when you are stressed out about finances. When you choose not to give the driver who cut you off the finger. When you choose to give the waitress an extra tip even though she messed up your order.

The treasure might appear in the form of a deep and meaningful relationship that you never knew was possible. The treasure might come from developing your character, growing as a person, becoming more and more like Jesus.

It is time to take up the job of being a treasure hunter instead of a field inspector. Stop focusing on the field or what is wrong with people. Turn your eyes toward the treasure—what God can do in that person or situation.

People are people and they are going to mess up. Here's a shocker: You are, too. So stop being mean. Quit being ugly. Be kind. Show grace. Love God and love people, even the ones who deserve and expect it the least.

## The Power of Kindness to Transform

Over the years, I have seen the power that comes from choosing to be kind, not just in my own family but in others.

I think of more than twenty years ago and my then personal assistant, Susan. Once she stopped focusing on the field of a husband who did not share her faith and started to be kind, she finally unearthed the treasure.

Susan was the first and only member of her family to be born again. For two years, she attended church alone. Every Sunday after service, she returned home to her husband and their twenty-year-old son, Tracy, neither of whom shared her faith. Her husband, Alan, was a good man and a good provider. He just was not interested in spiritual things. He would rather play golf and drink beer on Sundays.

Often Susan would leave a powerful atmosphere of praise and worship at church and go home to her husband and son, who were totally unspiritual. This affected her. It broke her heart. Many nights she cried herself to sleep, wondering if her family would ever be saved and share her faith.

After two years of coming to church by herself and living for God alone in their home, the Holy Spirit began to speak to her about how to win her husband for Christ. He challenged her to control her tongue. Susan began to show Alan respect, honor and unconditional love. Instead of being sad or bitter that she was the only Christian in her family, she came home from church, kissed her husband on the cheek and served him a delicious lunch. She did not play the victim, the poor little wife fighting the good fight of faith without her family's support. Nor did she judge Alan for not going to church or tell him he was a bad person. She showed kindness day in and day out.

Susan also prayed Ephesians 1:17–18 (CEV) over her husband every day:

> I ask the glorious Father and God of our Lord Jesus Christ to give you his Spirit. The Spirit will make you wise and let you understand what it means to know God. My prayer is that light will flood your hearts and that you will understand the hope that was given to you when God chose you. Then you will discover the glorious blessings that will be yours together with all of God's people.

Susan believed that God had a plan for her family, even though Satan was trying to convince her that Alan and Tracy would never get saved. But Susan kept believing, kept praying and kept being kind. She was witnessing to Alan without a word. Her gentle, kind spirit was witnessing to him.

As Alan watched the change in his wife, he started attending church with her. Even though he was not converted immediately, he sat beside his wife in service Sunday after Sunday. Their son observed his father going to church with his mother. A few weeks later, he, too, decided to check out the church.

That Sunday morning Tracy walked down the aisle, was born again and was filled with the Holy Spirit. A few weeks later I preached an illustrated sermon in which Tracy played one of the characters. When I gave the altar call that morning, Alan walked down the aisle and was gloriously saved and filled with the Holy Spirit.

God had an awesome assignment for this family. Today Tracy is a good friend who serves as the executive pastor over all our campuses. Alan is one of the greatest Christians I know.

I have heard that Mark Twain said, "Kindness is a language which the deaf can hear and the blind can see." Kindness can open doors of restoration. It can bring healing. It can tear down walls. It can offer hope. It can change people.

It does not matter if being kind does not come naturally in certain situations or if kindness feels like an interruption in your schedule. Do it anyway. And watch as God begins to mold your heart to love like you've never been hurt.

As this chapter ends, I would like to challenge you.

If you know anything about me, you know I am a huge advocate of fasting. This private discipline yields many personal benefits. It can change our lives and the lives of our families, our communities and even the world.

I want to challenge you to consider fasting from criticism. Do this for a minimum of 24 hours. Refrain from criticizing the government, your neighbor, the strangers who post on social media, your church or your spouse.

Proverbs 18:21 (MESSAGE) tells us, "Words kill, words give life; they're either poison or fruit—you choose." Negative words create an atmosphere that will suffocate or choke out a life-giving spirit.

Commit to speaking good things. And if you can't say anything nice, just don't say anything at all.

## THE BIG IDEA

Be kind—when you feel like it and when you don't.

# CHAPTER SEVEN

# FIGHTERS, FIRE STARTERS AND PEACEMAKERS

Boys, behave yourselves!" Dad's voice carried through the air to where my two brothers and I were making a ruckus. It seemed he was always telling us to stop fooling around. And, true to his character, he followed up the order by reminding us of the consequences if we disobeyed.

But boys will be boys.

I cannot remember exactly how it started. Maybe my brothers and I started wrestling in the bedroom, or we just continued the match our father had interrupted. However it began, it ended with a bang. Showing off his strength, one of my older brothers scooped up my little body in his arms and threw me into the wall. I crashed right through the drywall. It was kinda funny, seeing my body's imprint in the wall. The three of us gaped at the gigantic hole, eyes wide.

Dad, of course, did not think it was funny.

I heard my father holler at us to come into his bedroom. It was the moment of reckoning. I knew we deserved to be punished. And I planned on taking the whupping like a champ.

My father was a great man who always kept his emotions in control. I had never seen him lose his cool. Oh, he would get upset at us for misbehaving—and we always deserved his corrective words and whatever punishment he would dole out—but he certainly never disciplined us out of anger. I admired Dad for that.

This time was different. Looking back, I realize now we had probably nudged him to his breaking point, brought on by a culmination of the pressures of being a pastor, the financial weight of caring for a large family and trying to sort through difficulties with certain people at the church.

Dad reached for the belt as my two brothers and I lined up in front of him, three guilty parties. I knew I had earned what was coming, but Dad seemed a bit more angry than usual. Let me be clear: He did not whip us into oblivion or scream like a lunatic or anything when the leather strap came down. He was just mad.

After the three of us got our lashings, my brothers and I left the room. Sore and ashamed, we swore to ourselves that we would never, ever wrestle in the house again.

An hour later, while we were messing around with our G.I. Joes or something, Dad called out, "Boys, please come back in the room." My stomach sank. *Are we in more trouble? Wasn't one whupping enough?* My brothers and I exchanged bewildered glances and slowly trudged back into Dad's bedroom.

I will never forget the look on Dad's face. His eyes were red from crying and heavy with sorrow. I would wear the same expression as a father myself many years later.

I was confused. Had we done something wrong? And then came the most moving act of humility I had ever experienced from parent to child. As the four of us stood in a circle, Dad fell to his knees. Tears began to stream down his cheeks. Deep, gut-wrenching sobs poured out of his trembling body. "I'm so sorry," he stammered. "Your daddy did wrong. I lost my temper. I should not have done that to you."

Dad had always insisted that we apologize to one another, making us say "I'm sorry" for snatching away a toy or calling someone a name. But there in front of us, his knees cradled in the carpet, was a great man, our father, apologizing to us.

Even though I was a little boy, I knew in my heart it could not have been easy for him to admit he was wrong. That memorable picture of humility left a mark in our lives. It was a scene none of us would ever forget.

And then Dad took off his belt. He clenched it tight in his trembling hand as he gave it to one of us. "Here," he said. "Whip me."

My brothers and I stared at him, frozen. None of us would take it. Tears of our own streamed down our faces. There was nothing to do other than cry. My brothers and I reached forward and hugged Dad tight. The Spirit of God was in that room with us, wielding His power in a moment of forgiveness, of anger tempered, of lives forever changed.

Years later, I realized firsthand what my father had been going through. My own struggle of dealing with a child's rebellion and a house full of verbal battles that festered long after the last word was said—it was just too much.

I hated what this was doing to our family.

I hated what it was doing to me.


## Love Is Not Easily Angered

Do you remember a time when you lost control of your temper?

Maybe you yelled at your child, maybe even slipped in an expletive, and it frightened the living daylights out of her. Maybe you were already on edge when driving home from work; then someone cut you off and you started riding his bumper and screaming at him. Maybe after a few consecutive nights of little sleep, you blew up in a screaming fit at your spouse. Maybe you have gotten so out of control, you have done something physical, like thrown something at someone, punched a wall or smashed a window.

We have all been there to some degree. It is normal to get angry and to want to do something about it. But we cannot position ourselves to love like we've never been hurt if we are ruled by our tempers.

Ephesians 4:26 tells us, "And 'don't sin by letting anger control you.' Don't let the sun go down while you are still angry." Anger is not a sin. Mismanaging it is.

The next verse warns, "For anger gives a foothold to the devil." When we hold on to anger, when we nurture it, when we harp on it, when we think about it and dream about it, we give a place to the devil. The Greek word translated "place" or "foothold" is *topos*, which means "opportunity." It is also where we get the English word *topography*.

> **Anger is not a sin. Mismanaging it is.**

When we live with unresolved anger, the enemy gains ground in our hearts. We give the enemy authority. Just as the devil thrives in division, he also works well in an environment of anger. "For where envying and strife is, there is confusion and every evil work" (James 3:16 KJV).

Do not give the enemy any territory to set up camp.

Anger falls one letter short of danger. The best cure to manage your anger is delay. "He who is slow to anger is better than the mighty" (Proverbs 16:32 NKJV). One of the worst fruits of anger is revenge, as I talked about in chapter 4. Vengeance is a poor traveling companion. It is like biting a dog because the dog bit you.

When you seek vengeance, you are giving in to a desire to inflict harm and punishment on people who have wronged you. You wish them evil. You curse them. You might even want them dead. Vengeance is really the worst stage of unforgiveness; it will rob you of the creativity, positive energy and joy you need to live well.

God vows to take vengeance on His enemies; what is most critical for you is how you deal with your hunger for justice. So manage your anger. Be slow to respond. Keep your spirit in check.

> **"Human anger does not produce the righteousness God desires."**

The Bible teaches that "human anger does not produce the righteousness God desires" (James 1:20). Sometimes we try to solve our problems by unleashing anger. Truth is, that unruly emotion will never produce right behavior.

*Love is not easily angered.*

## Unguarded Moments

The pressures of life tend to bring out our rawest, deepest emotions. In those times, we are vulnerable to what I call an unguarded moment.

All it takes is a few minutes, even a few seconds, and you can lose your reputation, your testimony, your ministry or your relationships.

David almost lost his throne due to an unguarded moment—I'll get there in a minute. Allow me to share one of mine.

One evening when our children were young, I was bringing them home from a Wednesday night service. Cherise had gone out of town, and I had all five of the children by myself. On the drive home, they all started howling that they were starving.

We stopped at a fast-food joint with big initials. After I pulled up to the drive-through, I ordered five cheeseburger kids' meals, specifically and firmly requesting no onions and no pickles.

Back at home, the kids were tearing into their cardboard boxes and unwrapping their burgers when someone gasped in horror. "There's onions on mine!" Then another wailed, "There's pickles on mine!" Turns out every meal had pickles and onions. Kids being kids, they did not eat a thing. I threw all five unhappy meals in the trash and fed the kids cereal.

The following Wednesday, the kids and I headed to the same restaurant after the service. We pulled into the drive-through and I placed the same order. This time, I pleaded with the women speaking to me through the black box. "Please, ma'am, no onions and no pickles. This is extremely important. We asked for this last week, and it wasn't done. Please take care of it this week. No pickles or onions."

Of course, I was extremely nice about it. I am Pastor Franklin, after all. Not to mention, some of my members were in the line behind me!

The woman, whose voice I recognized from the week before, assured me she would handle it.

We made it home. The kids sat at the table, and I unwrapped cheeseburger number one. No onions and no pickles . . . and no meat! Nothing but a slice of cheese with a blob of ketchup and mustard graced the bun. I took out cheeseburger number two—ditto! Cheeseburger number three, same thing!

By now steam was whistling out of my ears and my eyes were rolling around in their sockets like the child in *The Exorcist*. I was ready to tell someone what they could do with those cheeseburgers.

I called the restaurant and demanded, "I want a manager! Who owns this restaurant? I want a name and number!" Some of the kids started cheering me on. "You go, Daddy! You get 'em!" About halfway through my tantrum, it dawned on me that I had just preached before hundreds of people, and now I was about to let somebody have it.

I immediately had to calm down. I realized I was having an unguarded moment.

Jesus said,

You have heard that our ancestors were told, "You must not murder. If you commit murder, you are subject to judgment." But I say, if you are even angry with someone, you are subject to judgment! If you call someone an idiot, you are in danger of being brought before the court. And if you curse someone, you are in danger of the fires of hell.

Matthew 5:21–22

Oops!

One unguarded moment can change your life.

It can make you lose your testimony. It can make you lose your anointing. It can make you lose your job. It can make you to go to prison. It can choke the move of the Holy Spirit in your life. It can close the door to miracles. It can sever the flow of blessings.

> **One unguarded moment can change your life.**

An unguarded moment almost cost David the throne.

## Who Tells You to Drop Your Sword?

Before David was crowned king of Israel, he was a fugitive in his own country. He was on the run from the reigning King Saul. Though David was anointed king during Saul's reign, he did not go to the throne immediately; he was anointed at seventeen but was not crowned until he was about thirty.

As his thirtieth birthday approached, the clock was ticking and none of God's promises had come to fruition in David's life. How can God say one thing but the circumstances of your life say otherwise?

Often, before you reach your destiny, you will experience the opposite of what you want. Not only that, but sometimes you will be tested right before you turn the corner to receive what God has promised.

Before David was to be crowned king of Israel, he and his band of rebels encamped on land owned by Nabal, a wealthy man. Nabal was married to a very beautiful and intelligent woman named Abigail. Although this man acted foolishly, his wife used her discernment to honor David, the man of God (see 1 Samuel 25).

David's men had decided to protect and guard Nabal's shepherds. Instead of asking for payment in money, they asked for food to replenish their strength.

Nabal acted just like his name, which means "foolish." He refused them any food. Adding insult to injury, he accused David of being a servant who had broken away from his master. In other words, he called David a nobody. By refusing David, Nabal insulted him.

When David's men reported what had transpired, David flipped out.

In this unguarded moment, he assembled four hundred of his fiercest warriors. "Strap on your swords, boys," he said. "We're going to get this Nabal. May God judge me if I don't kill him and every single male in his family before the sun sets."

How many of you have reached a breaking point in your life? Job stress, health problems, marriage problems, endless loads of thankless laundry, screaming children, unsympathetic bosses—then something happens that makes you lose it.

When pressure builds and our emotional and mental reserves are pushing empty, all it takes is one conversation, one poke at our already oozing wound, one person embarrassing us or one hurtful comment, and we can rip someone to shreds—maybe not physically, but through our words or spiteful actions.

Human emotion is unpredictable. And Christians are certainly not exempt from those times when life's pressures bring out our rawest, deepest emotions.

Think about this: What does your patience level look like when stress overwhelms? Or when the bank account is dwindling? Or when your teenagers are acting up? Or when the boss demands more time for less pay, again? Or when you are taking care of an elderly parent with Alzheimer's and you already feel drained taking care of your own young children? It is not so easy to squash fiery emotions in these situations.

When Abigail heard that David was coming to destroy her family, she did not crumble in the face of impending crisis. Instead, she prepared a picnic.

"A soft answer turns away wrath, but a harsh word stirs up anger" (Proverbs 15:1 NKJV).

Abigail carefully picked her timing and went to meet David. She whipped up an amazing meal of bread, wine, lamb and cake. She arrived and offered him and his men what she had prepared. She fed David, calmed him down and got him to relax.

God put Abigail in David's life to stop him from doing something that would kill his destiny. I find God always puts an Abigail in our lives. It can be a friend, a spouse, a pastor, the distraction of a phone call or even a child. And this Abigail will check you.

Maybe you have an Abigail in your life. If not, I want to introduce you to someone who will always be there for you: the Holy Spirit.

The Holy Spirit wants to intercept your unguarded moments.

Just when you are ready to let someone have it, the Holy Spirit can whisper in your ear, *Drop your sword.*

Whatever challenge is before you, know that it is a distraction designed for the enemy to edge you off-course from your destiny. If David had ignored Abigail's interception, it would have messed him up. And he would not have been crowned king of Israel.

> **The Holy Spirit wants to intercept your unguarded moments.**

Be aware of your unguarded moments.

Never respond to the ankle bites of a lesser man. Do not feel as though you have to get down on that same level. God will deal with people like this.

One amazing thing about this story is that Nabal died a few weeks later. David went on to marry Abigail, and he eventually became a great king. In saving David's future, this woman secured her own.

God took care of David's enemy. He wants to do the same for you. So when the argument breaks out, when someone makes your blood boil, when someone you love says something or does something that cuts you to the core, let the Holy Spirit step in. Let Him keep you from doing something stupid that will cost you your family, your dream or your destiny.

## Sometimes You Have to Zip It

There are times we are unable to physically withdraw from a situation, but we can drop our swords another way. We can shut our mouths.

We used to sing an old gospel song in church about how the Lord would fight our battles if we let Him, and we would always have the victory.

You do not need to argue with your enemy. You need to hold your peace and let the Lord fight your battle.

You do not need to tell off people who gossiped about you. You need to let God show them the error of their ways. You do not need to bark at your children because they did something stupid. You need to be still and let God work in their lives. You do not need to hurl a snappy comeback at your spouse after he or she said something hurtful. You can pray and say to yourself, "Be quiet, there's a victory in progress in my situation!"

> **You do not need to argue with your enemy. You need to hold your peace and let the Lord fight your battle.**

You probably know the story about how ancient Israel conquered the city of Jericho. It was not a result of their well-armed soldiers or their well-calculated battle strategies. God promised victory through an unusual means.

He commanded the people to march around the city once for six days, followed by seven times on the seventh day, during which the priests would blow their horns and the people would shout.

What is interesting—and many miss this crucial detail—is that before this happened, Joshua commanded the people, "Do not shout; do not even talk. . . . Not a single word from any of you until I tell you to shout. Then shout!" (Joshua 6:10).

In other words, shut up until I tell you otherwise.

How many times have you opened your mouth and caused destruction with the words that flew out? Maybe you cussed someone out, and in the same moment that first word slipped out, you knew it was wrong. Maybe you shouted hurtful remarks that long strained what was once a great friendship. Maybe you berated a loved one without any measure of self-control, and it scarred her sense of self.

Next time you are tempted to go to that place, be quiet. A miracle is in progress.

I like what Benjamin Franklin said: "Remember not only to say the right thing in the right place, but far more difficult still, to leave unsaid the wrong thing at the tempting moment."[1]

### Be a Peace Manufacturer

Jesus said, "God blesses those who work for peace, for they will be called the children of God" (Matthew 5:9). Another translation says, "Blessed are the peacemakers." I like the term *peace manufacturers*.

There comes a time when you should fight for what you believe. There comes a time to battle for your rights and sometimes for your very life.

But just as there is a time for war, there is also a time for peace (see Ecclesiastes 3:8).

Some of us are natural fighters. This is not always a bad thing, but it can be unhealthy. I'll admit, I am one of these people. If I really believe I am right on something, I will fight you to hell and back. Try to steal my boat, and I'll sink us both before I will let you have it.

Ask yourself this: When you find yourself in the middle of a volatile situation, how does your presence change things? Do you add kerosene to the roaring flames, or do you extinguish the fire?

I am sure you know someone who has a talent for stirring things up. If he pokes his head into a conversation you are having with a friend, he will quickly throw in his two cents, turn the volume on full blast and elevate the conversation to a heated level of crazy. It seems that everywhere he goes, trouble shows up.

Alternatively, a person who manufacturers peace will defuse situations. She will not stoke the flames—she will put out the fire. Think Abigail. Think Jesus.

Keep in mind that peace is not the absence of trouble. Peace does not mean that everyone will like you, or that you will never experience resistance. Peace is standing in the middle of a storm when lightning strikes a few inches away, thunder claps in your ear, your eyes are blurred by pounding rain, you can barely stand straight—but you choose to be still and not panic. You choose to trust God. You choose to be at peace in the midst of a storm.

> **Don't let strife infect you. Be a peace manufacturer.**

Don't let strife infect you. Be a peace manufacturer. Internal peace affects the external atmosphere.

So keep your peace when your spouse tries to pick fights. Keep your peace when your teenager says something mean to you. Keep your peace when someone gossips behind your back. Keep your peace when someone in the church spreads lies about you.

## Be at Peace When Others Won't

I am finally at peace with the fact that everybody is not at peace with me. It's not that I am mad at people or that I have intentionally offended them. It's just that not everyone likes or agrees with me. I am okay with this. I strive to be at peace with everyone, but the feeling is not always reciprocated. Not everyone is going to want to enter into peace with you.

Paul wrote, "If it is possible, as much as depends on you, live peaceably with all men" (Romans 12:18 NKJV).

Sometimes it is just not possible. There are moments our peace-manufacturer initiatives are not always successful. You can reach out and apologize to the cousin who has held a grudge against you for years, but she may refuse to let it go. You can speak peaceful words with your spouse, but your spouse may refuse to return the favor and continue to wage a war with divisive words. You can try to be at peace with your co-worker, but he may refuse to give you the time of day and choose instead to continue gossiping about you. Be at peace with the fact that not everyone is going to want to be at peace with you.

When Jesus sent out His disciples to preach and to heal people, He gave an interesting instruction. "Whenever you enter someone's home, first say, 'May God's peace be on this house.' If those who live there are peaceful, the blessing will stand; if they are not, the blessing will return to you" (Luke 10:5–6). Jesus was telling His crew that those who received the peace they offered would experience peace in their homes. If they refused, the peace offered would come in double portion back onto the disciples. Being a peace manufacturer is a win-win.

## The Pursuit of Peace

If you are going to have peace, you have to pursue it. Seek after peace. Be intentional about it. Here are a few practical steps to help you along the way.

First, tame your tongue. "A gentle answer deflects anger, but harsh words make tempers flare" (Proverbs 15:1). If you have nothing nice to say, don't say anything at all.

Second, do not jump into the struggle. When a family feud or a disagreement at work erupts, do not pick sides. Do not add to the conflict. Instead, pray about the situation and speak victory over it.

Third, keep a watch for whom you hang out with. When most of your friends are disgruntled, negative or critical, chances are you are going to end up like they are.

> **If you are going to have peace, you have to pursue it.**

Fourth, stop. Isaiah 26:3 says, "You will keep in perfect peace all who trust in you, all whose thoughts are fixed on you!" In other words, go to God with the situation and stop.

Allow the peace of Christ to rule in your heart. You were created to be a manufacturer of peace (see Colossians 3:15).

## THE BIG IDEA

Allow the Holy Spirit to guard your unguarded moments, and learn to be a peacemaker.

# CHAPTER EIGHT

# AND WE WERE ONE

**M**arriage was God's idea.

You can find it at the beginning and the end of God's designs for humanity. The first book of the Bible begins with a wedding in the Garden of Eden, that of Adam and Eve. The book of Revelation has near its end another wedding, the marriage supper of the Lamb.

Two are better than one.

Healthy marriages are still the way God builds His Church and exerts His influence over a lost and dying world. Know God has a purpose for your marriage. And He has a vested interest in seeing it succeed.

On the other side is an attack on family and marriage that cannot be denied. Our enemy has a very determined agenda, and destroying your marriage is high on his list of things to do.

Too many believers are losing this battle, not because it cannot be won, but because they cannot see the path to victory.

The good news is that for every marriage killer and for every mountain the enemy builds to discourage you, a Savior stands ready to protect you.

If you are striving to rekindle a connection with your spouse or are trying to hold on to what's left of your marriage, take heart. God can remove every mountain and deflect every arrow of the enemy. Remember, sometimes the greater the battle, the greater the victory.

**The greater the battle, the greater the victory.**

In our first season of marriage, Cherise and I found out just how different we were. It got so bad one day that my wife told her mother she wanted to come home.

Thank God for a godly mother-in-law! She told Cherise, "Absolutely not!" She exhorted both of us that we needed to stay in this and work through our differences. And she told us that we were being selfish. She was right, and over time Cherise and I worked through those things.

### Divorce: Not an Option

Over the years, I have learned the number-one core value Cherise and I share is that divorce will never be an option. That reality changes everything, especially the way you end an argument.

God could not be clearer about the commitment of marriage in the Bible—He hates divorce (see Malachi 2:16). It's that simple.

In Matthew 1:6, God wrote Uriah's name in Jesus' family tree when referring to Bathsheba as the mother of Solomon, who had also been Uriah's wife. By the time this text was written, Uriah was long dead, and so was David, who later legally became Bathsheba's husband. On top of that, when the prophet Nathan called out David for his sin after Uriah was killed, he also referred to Bathsheba as Uriah's wife, even though by then Bathsheba and David were married.

This makes me wonder if it is possible to be in a marriage that is recognized on earth but not in heaven. The question may offend some of you. I do not mean to condemn you if you are divorced.

God loves you and He forgives you. I simply want to challenge those who are married or are getting married to understand just how important a marriage commitment is.

Marriage is not a test run. God did not design this covenant for you to play house and hope for the best. Jesus tells us that outside of adultery, physical abuse or abandonment, we are called to stick it out . . . for better or for worse.

Cherise and I have a real marriage, and we lead real lives just like yours. We have had some real knock-down, drag-out arguments, just as you have. It is called being a human with a mind of your own. But we determined in our hearts a long time ago that in those times of disagreement, hurt or anger would not define us. Nor would they end our marriage. We were going to stick it out through thick and thin.

> **Marriage is not a test run.**

## A Cave of Couples

A remarkable passage of Scripture mentions a cave purchased by Abraham.

> Then Abraham bowed low before the Hittites and said, "Since you are willing to help me in this way, be so kind as to ask Ephron son of Zohar to let me buy his cave at Machpelah, down at the end of his field. I will pay the full price in the presence of witnesses, so I will have a permanent burial place for my family."
>
> Genesis 23:7–9

The Bible tells us that after Abraham bought this cave, he buried his wife in it when she died. Scripture also mentions that in addition to Sarah, Abraham, Isaac, Rebekah and even Jacob were all buried in this same cave.

*Machpelah*, the name of this cave, means "double." The cave of double—or the cave of couples.

How do we keep our marriages together and make it all the way to the cave of couples?

Adam and Eve are the first couple we can read about in the Bible. God made them the example for all other couples who choose to follow Him. After He had created man in His image, He declared, "It is not good for the man to be alone. I will make a helper who is just right for him" (Genesis 2:18). The King James Version uses the phrase *help meet.*

When God brought Eve to Adam, Adam said, "At last! This one is bone from my bone, and flesh from my flesh!" (verse 23). It is important to note that God did not give him another man. Nor did He give him three women. He made the first couple male and female.

God described Eve as a "help meet." I like to think of a help meet as someone who builds with divine help. This was the reason God created Eve—she was God's spiritual help for Adam in a divine package.

God looked at man and announced that the number-one need of man is not the need to breed. His number one need is divine help. If he is going to fulfill the call, purpose and plan of God for his life, he is going to need divine help.

### Your Divine Help

Women are multipliers and incubators. They increase anything you give them. If a man gives a woman a seed, she will incubate it, multiply it, increase it and nine months later give him back a baby. If he gives a woman his bachelor pad after he marries her, she will incubate it, multiply it and increase it. He gets furniture. He gets curtains. He gets more than just a house; he gets a home.

I am going to address men specifically in the next chapter, but for now I want you men to know this: You are going to win or lose your battles depending on whether you have divine help in your corner. You need divine help praying for you when you go to your job. You need divine help aiding you as you raise your children. You need divine help building that career and that business.

If you are a married man and do not have your wife in your corner, the divine help that you need will not be there. Imagine a time that you are able to celebrate something you have done that has become successful. If you begin ignoring or belittling your wife or acting as though you have accomplished it all by yourself, you need to stop and remember that she is your divine help sent by God.

Men, cherish your wives. Appreciate them. Love them. No matter what your relationship looks like right now, your wife will be your divine assistance. How you treat her will determine how God listens to your prayers.

Whatever little success I have had, the impact my wife has had on it has been profound, and some do not realize it. The truth is, without my wife's divine help, our ministry would not be here. And I certainly would not be writing this book.

I don't want a man cave. I want a couple's cave. I want to continue doing life with Cherise. Having friends and hobbies is important, but far more important is to make it to the cave of couples.

> Men, cherish your wives. Appreciate them. Love them. How you treat your wife will determine how God listens to your prayers.

Wives, I want to say that you are important. I will talk to you women more in the next chapter. For now, I want to tell you this: You matter. Your husband needs divine help in a human package, and you are that package. You can make a difference in whether your husband wins or loses in life because you are the divine help.

Psalm 127:1 says, "Unless the LORD builds a house, the work of the builders is wasted." When the Lord builds the house of a marriage, then the marriage is built to last. Each spouse is striving together, praying together, dreaming together, following the

Lord's will together, raising kids together and doing life together. This is the ultimate height you can reach in a marriage.

## How to Outlast Your Toughest Seasons

If you are going to make it in your marriage, you have to learn some secrets for outlasting your toughest times. What do you do when your 401(k) has fallen like an egg from a tall chicken? What do you do when you have been laid off and you have no income? What do you do when your spouse is afflicted by depression or illness? What do you do when your family is under siege? How do you love your spouse as if he or she has never hurt you?

I love to study David in the Bible because he was a multidimensional person. He was not always happy. He experienced a full range of emotions and dealt with plenty of highs and lows. One moment he was on top of the world; in the next, he felt as if the world was caving in on him.

You can hit a season of marriage in which everything is going so well that it makes all the little problems you have seem like nothing. I have found it is the tough seasons, though, that define what "tough" is. During this time, your perspective changes. I once saw a pastor illustrate this point by getting down on the floor and lying prostrate. When you are that low, everything looks different, out of order, even, and larger than it does when you are standing up straight.

If you are facing a battle in your marriage—whether you and your spouse cannot get on the same page concerning an important issue, or you are dealing with a wayward child, or you are struggling with illness, addiction or financial problems—I have good news. God's justice and His mercy are such that He sets an end to the darkness (see Job 28:3).

You are going through a season. You have not been handed a sentence.

I would like to offer four keys to help you love your spouse during these tough times.

### 1. Go through the valley of trouble together.

Here's the deal: In marriage, you are going to get mad and be angry at one another. You are going to offend and get offended. You are going to hear harsh words and speak them. You are going to get on your spouse's last nerve, and your spouse will do the same to you.

When we go through the valley of trouble, we do not grab our toothbrushes, head out the door and say it's over. We reach over, grab each other's hand and keep pursuing God.

Even in the lowest seasons of marriage, God will always open a door of hope. I do not care how bad it gets. I do not care how dark it gets. I do not care how many demons you're fighting. I do not care how much sin has come into your home. There is a door of hope in every valley of marital trouble.

Research shows that, statistically, the happiest couples are those who have been married thirty to thirty-five years. It typically takes the first nine to seventeen years for people to die to self. That is why the highest percentage of divorces occur during the first nine years of marriage.

> There is a door of hope in every valley of marital trouble.

You need to understand that some days are good and some days are tough. You must determine to stick it out together.

### 2. Go deeper.

I love meeting newlyweds. I do not want to lose that same fresh, romantic bond with Cherise. But feelings do not last. The only way any of us are going to hold it together in life and with each other is to keep going deeper and deeper into Jesus. Grow your faith as a couple. Pray together. Read the Bible together. Worship together.

When life happens, when storms come, when offenses come, when feelings get hurt, we have something greater to hold us together. We do not let trials, troubles, issues and problems stop us. We go deeper in God.

Jesus is the answer. Whatever is troubling your marriage, He can handle it.

> **Determine to walk out your tough season together, all the way to the cave of couples.**

Determine to walk out your tough season together, all the way to the cave of couples. No quitting. No giving up. Go deeper in Jesus, no matter what life brings.

### 3. Believe in your destiny as a couple.

As soon as David was anointed king of Israel by Samuel, he began to face battles. His brothers rejected him. A lion tried to kill him, followed by a bear. Then came Goliath. The reigning king, Saul, got jealous and tried to kill him. When Saul failed, his army chased David for years. The battles never stopped.

All of these problems seemed daunting and unfair to David. But a spiritual truth was at work that he simply could not see. David was not suffering a series of injustices and unfortunate events. Rather, God was preparing David to be king. David was training for reigning.

The same principle applies to your life. You have not gone through what you have gone through because of a series of unfortunate coincidences . . . ever. God has been preparing you for your assignment. God is taking you higher.

Every marriage goes through the delight stage, and every marriage goes through the disillusionment stage. But if you will hold on, if you will keep loving one another, if you will lead in forgiveness, humility and honesty, you will move from the delight phase through the disillusionment phase to the ultimate destiny phase of a marriage.

If I had married any other girl in the world, I would have missed the destiny God had for Cherise and me. She had to be the one. God put her with me and me with her. I believe marriage is more than just two people falling in love. When God is truly in the center of a marriage, destiny is attached to it. My children have a destiny. My family has a destiny. Our church was waiting on Cherise and me, and that was our destiny.

> **God honors commitment. Every time you make a vow, you must honor that vow.**

God honors commitment. Every time you make a vow, you must honor that vow. It matters. Even if the circumstances were not right when you and your spouse came together, you must still honor your marriage vows.

The destiny of your marriage is at stake. The destiny of your children's future is at stake. The destiny of God's purpose for your life is at stake.

### 4. Don't give up.

Don't lose your way. Don't fall aside. God has not left you unprepared for your tough season.

If you are going through a challenging time, if you are wondering if you will ever love your spouse the same way again, hold on. If you do not give up and if you work on your marriage, God will meet you there and make a way—even when there seems to be no way.

You and I have freezers in our homes. You put things in there that you want to eat later. You do not stow food items away because they are not valuable or you don't want them. You just want them at another time.

The same is true in our walk with God. If you are going through a deep freeze, and it feels like you are forsaken by God, it is not that God does not love you. He is just saying, *Later—not now.* *You're going to move into another season, and I'm getting you ready for it. You're going to hit levels you have never hit before and do things you have never done before. You are going to know joy like you have never known joy before! You are going to dream dreams you have never dreamed before! But it's later, not now.*

Don't give up on your spouse. Don't give up on your marriage. God has big plans for you and the one you married!

## THE **BIG** IDEA

There is a door of hope in every valley of marital trouble.

# CHAPTER NINE

# FIGHT FOR YOUR MARRIAGE

A dultery is more of a reality in our modern-day world than it has ever been. Widely accepted in the world, it floods our subconsciousness through television and social media. It may be considered normal, but it is far from harmless.

I recently got ahold of a book called *Sexual Detours* by Dr. Holly Hein. In it, she gives some astonishing statistics: Seventy percent of men will cheat on their wives. Sixty percent of women will cheat on their husbands.[1]

Under the marriage covenant, two become one. You cannot violate the covenant through adultery without devastating both parties to some degree. Though infidelity can certainly be forgiven, scars are permanent. I have never counseled an individual through a crisis of adultery who did not deeply regret his or her decision to be unfaithful.

If you have been cheated on, you know the pain of infidelity. It hurts. It shatters trust. It severs relationships. It degrades people. It destroys families. Marriage is about giving; adultery is about taking. This is why the Bible is clear that adultery is a sin.

If adultery has infected your marriage, you may wonder how on earth you can love your spouse the same. Or even again.

Though one of the biblical grounds for divorce is adultery, this does not mean divorce is always the right answer. In chapter 4 I talked about our need to forgive and set healthy boundaries. In the context of infidelity, while you must forgive your spouse for this betrayal, you can choose to stay married under these circumstances or not. Either way, you must forgive the infidelity.

> **Though infidelity can certainly be forgiven, scars are permanent.**

When your spouse cheats on you, you enter a crisis of identity. You wonder if you can ever trust this person again. You wonder if the marriage can even survive. Of course, the easiest solution is divorce. The hardest is to stay and turn crisis into an opportunity. An opportunity? Yes, that's right. Every affair has an opportunity to redefine a relationship. Though an affair will produce hurt and betrayal, on the flip side, it can also produce room for growth, reflection and reevaluation of the relationship.

Look, when certain things happen in a marriage, the marriage will not be the same. If you have been wounded by betrayal of the worst kind, the relationship may be over. At least the way that it was.

Are you willing to consider a second marriage with the same person?

## How to Affair-Proof Your Marriage

Sex is very powerful, and unless it is kept in the confines of marriage, it can explode with a power destructive enough to tear apart families.

Earlier I mentioned that 70 percent of men will cheat on their wives and 60 percent of women will cheat on their husbands.

If you are blessed not to be in either of those two percentages, I would like to give you five ways to affair-proof your marriage.

### 1. Get it out of your head.

Adultery begins on the stage of imagination. Before the enemy gets you in the bed, he has to get in your head. The temptation to cheat begins with one thought.

This is what Jesus was talking about when He discussed the problem of a person lusting through his eyes. Jesus said you cannot control your wandering eye: "Pluck it out" was his suggestion (Matthew 5:29). Of course, He was not making a literal command. Jesus was saying the problem is not the eye but the heart.

Plucking out your eye means canceling your subscription to *Playboy*, getting rid of certain channels on your television and not clicking on certain websites. Pluck things out that may cause you to stumble out of your marriage. The enemy is creeping into homes through the eye gate and through technology. I believe this is the number-one threat to most marriages today.

> **The enemy is creeping into homes through the eye gate and through technology. I believe this is the number one threat to most marriages today.**

Adultery always begins with thoughts that can lead to actions that destroy your life. Watch your words because they become thoughts. Watch your thoughts because they become actions. Watch your actions because they become habits. Watch your habits because they become character. Watch your character because it controls your destiny.

### 2. Respect one another.

Be more interested in taking responsibility and fixing whatever problem you have than avoiding blame. Do you want to be reconciled or do you want to be right?

### 3. Take responsibility.

Philippians 2:4 (ESV) tells us, "Let each of you look not only to his own interests, but also to the interests of others." Major problems in marriage come from one foul word—selfishness.

I did not feel that selfishness was an issue when I was single. I have learned over the years that, like all great challenges in life, marriage does not make you who you are; it reveals who you are. It is what we do with what we learn about ourselves that makes us more tender or harder of heart.

Selfishness lies at the core of every marital problem. I wish I could tell you twenty ways to avoid being selfish, but it is a heart matter. It is deeply engrained through our habits and our routines.

This is where your relationship with the Lord comes in. When you draw near to God, it produces a mirror that reveals what you really look like to others . . . and to God, because He always sees what is true. Take time to pray and read your Bible. Plant yourself in God's house, and soon the rough edges will be revealed as God does a transformational work in your life. The goal is always to look less like you and more like Jesus.

### 4. Rekindle the romance.

If more formality and even old-fashioned "courting" were present in marriages, fewer marriage partners would wind up in court. Remember how kind and tender you were to each other when you were dating? Back then it was fun. You anticipated every date with excitement. If we don't watch out, the fun goes right out of our marriage. We need to cultivate romance again. Start a weekly date night. Get away for the weekend. Find a way to reconnect with the one you love.

### 5. Have a made-up mind.

Trying times are not the times to stop trying. When tough times come and you are tempted to flirt with that co-worker, remember the words you said before God: "For better, for worse; for richer, for poorer; in sickness and in health; to love and to cherish."

Marriage has to endure storms. That will require great resolve. The enemy will do everything he can to destroy your marriage, your family and your purity. It is not just a battle over you and your wife; it's about your children and your children's children.

Leonardo da Vinci is purported to have said something I love to remember: "An arch consists of two weaknesses which, leaning one against the other, make a strength." That's what mar-

> **Trying times are not the times to stop trying.**

riage is. The starting point of a powerful marriage is when you acknowledge, "God, I need You. God, without You, I am selfish. I will not do what I should do and be what I should be."

I made up my mind many years ago that my family would never have to walk around this town and hear people snicker because their daddy could not keep his zipper up or because he could not live a life that would bring honor and glory to Jesus Christ.

A committed and lasting marriage demands a made-up mind. You must be deliberate. You must resolve not to commit adultery.

When it comes to our marriages, we must be on guard. We must proactively protect the gift God has given us. In order to do this, we must respect one another, take responsibility for our actions, romance our partners and resolve to stand amidst the storms life throws our way.

## For You Men

I want to speak to the men reading this. Women, you can read, too, of course, but this section is specifically designed to awaken and encourage men.

Men are called to be the leaders in the home. This is not a chauvinistic order, it is a godly one. Many women, perhaps some of you reading this, are single moms, and I applaud you for raising your children on your own. You may not have a husband who will take responsibility for the spiritual condition of your family, and you have accepted the task. Thank you for that. But it is time for men to start standing up and being held accountable for what goes on under their roofs.

Men, you are probably well aware that marriage in the 21st century is no easy matter. You may be taking in what I've written and feel discouraged. Maybe you feel the weight of the world on your shoulders. Or that you and your wife had one fight too many this past year. Or that your relationship is in a deep freeze. Or that you do not even know the woman you married five or fifteen years ago.

I want to encourage you to be strong and courageous.

You may feel as if you're running on empty, but stand up for your marriage. Stand up in the middle of the junk you are facing and determine to lead your wife well.

One of my favorite Scriptures is Joel 3:9 (NKJV): "Prepare for war! Wake up the mighty men, let all the men of war draw near, let them come up." Do you consider yourself a mighty man who is leading the spiritual charge in your home?

Sadly, the odds do not favor homes led by mighty men. According to a Pew Research Center study, more women than men say religion is very important to them (60 percent versus 47 percent). More women pray daily than men (64 percent versus 47 percent). More women attend religious services at least once a week (40 percent versus 32 percent).[2] You do not have to read a study to see evidence of this, though. Just visit a local church and you will see that women outnumber men.

A disconnect exists between men and church. I am not going to condemn you men for not going to church or slacking on your spiritual responsibilities to the family. Rather, I want to encourage you to pick the mantle up and start running. To keep things simple, here are four principles to help you become a mighty man in your home.

- *Play the man.* Lead, don't follow. God has given you charge over your family. This is your job, so lead your family well. Honor your wife. Set an example for your children.

  Watch what is happening under your roof, in the bedrooms, on the TV, on the computer, on the phones, on the tablets and devices. Get control of your anger. You do not have a right to be unkind to anyone who lives under your roof (or anywhere else). Get your desires and your urges under control. Become self-disciplined. Do not just do whatever you want whenever you want. Live by a set of standards spiritually and personally.

  > Play the man. Lead, don't follow.

  Communicate to your wife and your children in more than one-word sentences. Your wife or your kids may talk a lot. I get it; I have four daughters. But it does not entitle you to grunt your responses or retreat to a man cave instead of having a conversation with them. Quit growling and start talking.

- *Be the watchman.* Pay attention to your family. There should be no such thing as privacy. See who is doing what on social media or on the internet. Get off your phone. Get off your couch. Get out of your office. Become the watchman of your family.

- *Stand firm in the faith.* In 1 Corinthians 16:13 (NKJV), Paul says, "Watch, stand fast in the faith, be brave, be strong." Hold tight to what you believe about God and the Bible. Do not start changing your theology because you have lowered the standard and lost your convictions. Go to church with your family. Lead them in prayer.

- *Finally, let all you do be done in love.* "Love without stopping" (1 Corinthians 16:14 MESSAGE). The only thing that will produce righteousness in your home is to love without stopping.

Forgive again. Say you are sorry again. Speak words of encouragement and blessing over your wife, even if you do not feel like it.

Being a husband and a father can get messy. I have days when I am mean and ugly. I have days when things get on my nerves a lot easier than other days. When I am under pressure, I sometimes take it out on those I love the most. I hate it, but I just do.

I recently had one of those weak moments. I could feel negativity creeping in, but then I heard the Lord speak to me: *Here's what I have called you to do as a father. You have two responsibilities: Number one, make sure that your family has a relationship with God, through Jesus Christ. And number two, pour into them self-esteem through affirmation.* In other words, love without stopping.

Men, pray for God to help you lead well.

Marriage today requires an extraordinary commitment, but that does not come without help from a God who is for you and who is with you and who will provide what you need, exactly when you need it, if you will simply call out His name. He is your very present help in times of trouble. He is your strong tower. And He is for you. Play the man . . . and trust the rest to Jesus.

## For You Women

Your turn, women.

If you are going to keep your marriage together and raise godly children, you need the help of God. We all do!

Your home is a classroom, and you are the teacher. The question is, will your marriage or your family pass the grade? If you are not sure, you need to give yourself and your relationship to God today. You cannot successfully build a marriage without the power of the living God flowing through you. You need a clear mission of victory for your marriage. You must have a sure foundation, and that foundation is Jesus Christ!

Proverbs 31 paints the portrait of a godly wife and mother. We read, "Who can find a virtuous and capable wife? She is more precious than rubies" (Proverbs 31:10). Your virtue is what makes you priceless, ladies!

I find it interesting that before the names of hurricanes and tropical storms rotated between male and female, storms were only given female names. There is a lesson worth noting.

God wants every woman to understand the powerful ability He has placed inside of her. Inside of you! Women have the capacity to bring rest into their homes. You can bring chaos or you can bring peace. You can bring turmoil or you can bring calm. Have you ever heard the saying, "If Mama ain't happy, ain't nobody happy"? That is the truth! The book of Proverbs reveals this power: "Every wise woman builds her house, but the foolish one tears it down with her own hands" (Proverbs 14:1 AMPC).

When you love like you've never been hurt, you create a life-giving atmosphere in your home. I know this may seem hard to do if your husband works too much overtime, or not at all. Or when you are in a season of diapers and no sleep. Or when it feels as if you and your husband have lost that lovin' feeling.

Here are three keys to help you through this process:

- Remember you are the doorway to spiritual life in your marriage. Read the verses below so you can grasp what I am saying:

  > It is better to dwell in a corner of the housetop [on the flat oriental roof, exposed to all kinds of weather] than in a house shared with a nagging, quarrelsome, and faultfinding woman.
  >
  > Proverbs 21:9 AMPC

> A quarrelsome wife is like a constant dripping on a rainy day; restraining her is like restraining the wind or grasping oil with the hand.
>
> Proverbs 27:15–16 NIV

Enough tearing down your husband. Stop complaining. Quit the negative talk. It is up to you to build up your home. You can usher in the peace or you can usher in the storm. Choose to be the peacemaker.

- *Watch what you say.* In your tongue is the "law of kindness" (see Proverbs 31:26). In other words, don't be a hell-raising, potty-mouthed woman. Use your words to produce happiness and lift your husband's spirit. Remember, a kind word will go further every time than a word said in haste or anger.
- *Build up your husband.* Proverbs 14:1 says, "A wise woman builds her home, but a foolish woman tears it down with her own hands."

You are a fool if you do not build up your husband. When is the last time you thanked him for doing something? When is the last time you called him a good man? When is the last time you cut him some slack instead of nagging him to take out the garbage or turn the game off?

> You can usher in the peace or you can usher in the storm. Choose to be the peacemaker.

I know your husband is not perfect. But, ladies, he was not perfect when you married him! Instead of telling your man everything that is wrong with him, let God show him. Your job is to encourage him. Be grateful for him. Show him respect. Believe in him.

## Fight for What's Left

A pastor friend of mine spoke at the funeral of a seventeen-year-old boy who was killed by a drunk driver. The mother of the child was sitting on the front row next to her two remaining children. Her grief was unspeakable.

In this challenging situation for a pastor, my friend shared the story of a woman named Rizpah in the Bible. Rizpah had two sons. During a time of famine, both of her sons were handed over to the Gibeonites as punishment for their father breaking a covenant of peace. The Gibeonites put them to death by hanging.

As their lifeless bodies swung in midair, Rizpah took a bat and beat away the wild animals and vultures trying to pick at the decaying bodies of her sons. She pitched a tent and stayed there for three months, even though her boys were already dead. Rizpah fought for a proper burial for her sons. Finally, when word reached the king, he cut down what was left of the young men and buried their remains in a tomb reserved for royalty.

The enemy may have devastated you or your marriage. Your spouse may have cheated on you. Your spouse may have said or done something hurtful or shocking.

Fight for what's left.

God can heal your marriage. God can restore your marriage. God can renew your marriage.

Fight for what's left.

The enemy may have attacked your marriage, but perfect marriages don't make it to the cave of couples. The marriages that do have been through hell, but through the grace of God they have declared, "We will fight for what's left!"

> The enemy may have attacked your marriage, but perfect marriages don't make it to the cave of couples.

God can give you the grace to recover it all. He can restore what the enemy tried to take from you. If you give God your marriage, with all the lies, the lust and the baggage that comes with it, He can touch your relationship with grace and turn you and your spouse into winners. God can bless and anoint your marriage. You do not have to give up, and you do not have to quit.

We are all deeply flawed. We all mess up. We all make mistakes. We all say cruel things and do stupid things. But we have to declare to ourselves and to our spouses, "You and I are going to make it. We are going to end up in the cave of couples."

Fight for what's left.

## When in Doubt, Say the Following

The four hardest statements to make in marriage are these:

1. I was wrong.
2. I am sorry.
3. Forgive me.
4. I need help.

Need some great advice? Use them often.

(One of my favorite lines is, "I do not know what I was thinking." Feel free to take it!)

Half the people I grew up with are now divorced, while at the time of writing this book, Cherise and I celebrated our thirtieth wedding anniversary. We have a history together. Sure, we have had rough patches. Some people glide into marital bliss, but we have had to work our way there. We have had arguments that lasted too long, and we have gotten stuck in places that we should have moved forward in. But at the end of the day, my wife and I have decided "till death do we part."

I am thankful to have a family that is intact. It is not perfect, but it is intact. That means that my children can go to one set of parents. I do not say that harshly to those who have been divorced. If you have been divorced, God loves you. Stay open. He has a plan for you. But I am thankful that we stayed together because our kids have witnessed a marriage that was not perfect at all but that made it through the struggles.

Tension might fill your marriage. Maybe recently one of you mentioned the word *divorce*. Maybe you just found out your spouse did something that broke your heart. Marriage is still a good idea. Your marriage is still the most important part of your life. Your marriage is still worth the time it takes to do it right.

God has a plan, and it is my prayer that you and your spouse begin by renewing your commitment to God and to first and foremost growing in your faith.

There are no marriage plans designed to bring you to the cave of couples that do not involve you growing in your faith and in your relationship with Jesus Christ. Start there. He will guide you in the rest and prove to be a strong tower in times of trouble and a faithful Father in all seasons of life.

## THE BIG IDEA

The enemy may have attacked your marriage, but perfect marriages are not the ones that make it to the cave of couples. The marriages that do have been through hell, but through the grace of God they have declared, "We will fight for what's left!"

# CHAPTER TEN

# A FOUNDATION THAT LASTS

You probably are familiar with the most notorious family feud in American history: the one between the Hatfield and McCoy families. Beginning in the late nineteenth century and continuing for generations, these two clans were at war with one another. A total of eighteen family members died during the violent-at-times conflict.

It is said that the bad blood erupted in 1878 over a stolen pig. The case eventually went to court, and the Hatfields won. The fuel of an interfamily romance stoked the fires of hatred between the two Appalachian families. The inevitable murders occurred on both sides, and in their aftermath, the feud made its way to the U.S. Supreme Court in 1888.

This familial conflict is so embedded in pop culture that it is believed to be the inspiration for the popular game show *Family Feud*. Three years after the show first aired in 1976, both families were featured on TV playing against each other.

The families announced a truce in 1891 but did not shake hands on it until 1976. Finally, in 2003, in a public, televised event aired by the CBS network, the two families signed a formal truce. Reo Hatfield explained that "after Sept. 11 he wanted to make an official statement of peace between the two families to show that if the most deep-seeded family feud can be mended, so can the nation unite to protect its freedom."[1]

These long-standing hostilities remind me of what the Bible calls in Ezekiel 25:15 "old hatred" (KJV). This Scripture refers to the conflict between the people of Israel and the Philistines, which had endured for generations. Sometimes families will hold on to offenses that happened so long ago they forget why they are still mad. All they can think is, "My grandma hated them. My mama hated them. So I hate them."

*Old hatred.* Definitely not how we learn how to love like we've never been hurt.

## A Godly Family

God is in the business of blessing families. He has a purpose for them. He has a plan for them. He wants to use them. If the echoes of slammed doors and shouting voices are ringing in your ears, these truths might be hard for you to read.

> God is in the business of blessing families.

Still, they're true.

Family brings trouble. It brings challenge. It brings crisis. It brings hurt. Yet the family is still God's plan and His idea.

The devil is out to destroy our families. And he will work every angle and in every corner to make that happen.

God is calling you to lead your family in love and by love. Pray. Do the right thing.

Nowhere else in this life will you find greater fulfillment and love than within the heart of your family. Family is worth pursuing and fighting for. Do not give up on your loved ones. Go after them with the same love and grace and mercy with which God pursues you.

My wife is a general contractor. She builds homes, including the one we live in today. Just before the construction workers poured the concrete foundation for our house, Cherise and I did something a bit unusual. We put a Bible in a plastic bag and placed it in the dirt. It was a symbolic gesture of our commitment to build that house on the right foundation. Because its strength is not in the house itself. The pretty wall colors, the kitchen fixtures and the fancy wood flooring in your home are not going to protect you from storms. But the foundation will.

What foundation is your home built on?

## Build the Right Foundation

For more than thirty years, the small town of Imperial Beach in California welcomed hundreds of thousands of visitors from around the world one weekend each summer for their annual U.S. Open Sandcastle Competition. Complementing the sparkling blue ocean waters was a shoreline dotted with hundreds of competitors working their artistic magic, using sand.

Beginning early in the morning, men and women used buckets, straws and shovels to create cartoon characters, mythical creatures, replicas of historical sculptures and monuments and, of course, intricately designed castles. For hours, they would shuffle back and forth from ocean to dry land refilling buckets of water. Competitors watered the sand, packed the sand and shaped the sand in a labor of love requiring amazing detail and patience.

By four in the afternoon, these jaw-dropping sand sculptures had been admired by visitors, judged by experts and awarded prizes. Then came the tide. At first, it would stretch merely inches beyond the present shoreline. Slowly, as the minutes passed, the tide would roll farther and farther toward the sandy beach.

Grain by grain, each breathtaking and carefully constructed work of art began to dissolve. Foundations were washed away by the descent of foam-topped waves until, finally, each of the hundreds of sculptures was swept into the endless ocean.

Jesus said,

> Anyone who listens to my teaching and follows it is wise, like a person who builds a house on solid rock. Though the rain comes in torrents and the floodwaters rise and the winds beat against that house, it won't collapse because it is built on bedrock. But anyone who hears my teaching and ignores it is foolish, like a person who builds a house on sand. When the rains and floods come and the winds beat against that house, it will collapse with a mighty crash.
>
> Matthew 7:24–27

Storms are going to come. If you have not been through any yet, trust me, one is coming. It does not matter how much Scripture you have memorized, how much you have tithed, how long you have served at your church or how long you spend in prayer—it rains on the just and the unjust.

**Jesus is the only foundation that can secure your life, your home, your marriage and your family against the inevitable tides.**

Jesus is the only foundation that can secure your life, your home, your marriage and your family against the inevitable tides. No other foundation is going to stand.

I have talked about how important it is to firmly establish your faith and continually deepen it as a leader of your household. The goal is to pass on this legacy of faith to your family. The only way you can do this is to build a foundation in Jesus. This means that even when your baby is in the hospital, the doctor says the cancer is coming back, your teenage daughter runs away or you find porn on the computer, you can believe that when the storm is over, your house will stand.

When you think you cannot love the husband who failed, the mother who abused you or the child who stole your money, remember that the Rock you build your house on is stronger than the sin. The Rock is stronger than the rebellion. The Rock is stronger than the iniquity. The Rock is stronger than the addiction.

See, sand castles are easy to build. And they're fun to make. The sun shines, the weather is perfect, a light breeze is hitting your back. Everyone around you is laughing and having a great time. Building a brick house, on the other hand, takes blood, sweat and tears. And time—a lot more time. But unlike sand castles, they last.

Think of the foundation you are building for your family. When your faith is secure in Jesus, you will learn to love like you've never been hurt. You can forgive the betrayal. You can let go of the offense. You can stand when your child says she hates you. You can keep believing God will pull through when everything around you is crumbling.

Build a strong foundation. Turn off the distractions of the world, the computer, the TV, the negative people, the negative thinking. Tune into the right things. Spend time in prayer. Meditate on the Word. Allow the Holy Spirit to speak into and move in your life. Go to church. And do these things when the tide comes in, because that is the only way your family will stay standing.

## Pass on the Garment of Faith

The book of Exodus offers instructions concerning the high priests of Israel. Stay with me while I unpack this a bit.

> Then take the vestments and dress Aaron in the tunic, the robe of the Ephod, the Ephod, and the Breastpiece, belting the Ephod on him with the embroidered waistband. Set the turban on his head

and place the sacred crown on the turban. Then take the anointing oil and pour it on his head, anointing him. Then bring his sons, put tunics on them and gird them with sashes, both Aaron and his sons, and set hats on them. Their priesthood is upheld by law and is permanent. . . . Aaron's sacred garments are to be handed down to his descendants so they can be anointed and ordained in them.

Exodus 29:5–9, 29 MESSAGE

When Aaron, the first high priest of Israel, died, a curious thing happened. According to Numbers 20, this was right after the people of Israel journeyed from Kadesh to Mount Hor. Aaron was an old man by this time, and he was dying. God spoke to Moses, Aaron's brother, and gave him a strange directive: "Take Aaron and his son up the mountain. Take Aaron's clothes off and put them on his son. Then Aaron will die" (see Numbers 20:25–26).

God wanted Aaron's son to wear the same exact garment that his father wore when he served as high priest. What does this mean? This was God's way of saying, "I'm calling this family. I'm placing a special anointing upon this family. Something is different about them. They are not like others; they are unique. I have a special purpose for them."

This sounds like a nice benediction for ancient times. But what does it have to do with our families now?

According to 1 Peter 2:9, we—meaning every believer in Christ—are a "royal priesthood." We are not like the other families in our cul-de-sac or in our community. We are a priesthood family. We are called. We are anointed.

Think about the garments you put on every day as you go about your business. What do you wear? What kind of garment are you passing down to the next generation?

Are you passing down a garment of peace or a garment of contention?

A garment of prayer or a garment of bickering?

A garment of needing to be right or a garment of striving toward reconciliation?

A garment of forgiveness or a garment of bitterness?

A garment of kindness or a garment of frustration?

A garment of faith or a garment of worry?

A garment of loving like you've never been hurt or a garment of resentment for all the pain you've endured?

**What kind of garment are you passing down to the next generation?**

We will pass on to our kids only what we wear, not what we profess. I can say that Jesus is the priority in my life, but if my family never sees me wearing that priority Monday through Saturday, then it does not matter. I will not pass on what I said. I will only pass on what I wear.

It seems the true colors and depth of our faith and character are revealed during tough times. I will go so far as to say that only during these seasons do we see clearly what garments we are wearing.

What happens when we get the dreaded phone call, when we are holding the pen to sign the divorce papers, when the CT scan shows the cancer has spread, when the abuse happens, when injustice comes?

Think about what you are passing down to your family, to your children and even to theirs, during these moments of crisis. Are you modeling the power of faith to your children by seeking God, or do you fall to pieces and run to any and every secular source in search of peace?

If you are reading this right now and are not happy about the garment you are wearing, don't be discouraged. You might feel like a failure because your family is going through a crisis. You might feel like giving up. You might think you messed up too badly. You might think you have gone too far. You might think the wounds are too deep. You might think you are the only one. I'm here to tell you that it is not too late.

No family is perfect. No person is perfect. You can change course today. You can turn the tide. You can begin to put on a garment of faith that has been through trials and tribulations and pressure like you never could have imagined but that stands strong, that resists temptation, that does what is right.

If you want to pass on the "garment of faith" to your children, then start wearing it, and wear it well!

The enemy cannot have our families. He cannot have our homes. He cannot have our children. When we wear the right garments—the garments of praise, holiness, purity and supernatural anointing—no weapon formed against us will prosper!

God wants to restore your home. He wants to heal your broken relationships. He wants to give you peace. He wants to give you hope. He wants to restore what you have lost, what has been stolen, even what you have trashed.

God wants to show you how to love like you've never been hurt.

## Four Ways to Love Like You've Never Been Hurt

You have a responsibility as a parent to lead your family well. The following four steps will help you love them even when it feels impossibly hard:

1. Pray.
2. Stay committed.
3. Be aware of your greatest temptation.
4. Say "I'm sorry"—and mean it.

### Step 1: Pray

Never stop praying for your children.

As long as we have breath, we are to pray for them. Our kids cannot soar without our prayers. They cannot reach the high places without our prayers. We will only see the hand of God move in their hearts and on their lives with our faithful prayers.

If your teenager refuses to talk to you, pray. If your daughter won't have anything to do with you, pray. If your son is rebelling against you, pray. If your relationship with an adult child is strained, pray.

Pray without ceasing.

### Step 2: Stay Committed

After serving for 22 years as president of Columbia Bible College and Seminary (now Columbia International University), John Robertson McQuilkin resigned. He gave up a successful career so he could care full-time for his wife, who was stricken with Alzheimer's disease.

Years earlier, when Muriel was first diagnosed, McQuilkin mentioned to the school's board that he would eventually need to step down. They understood but never made any movement to find a replacement.

When Muriel's condition deteriorated, McQuilkin began to wrestle with the decision to institutionalize her. It made sense on paper. Even colleagues and trusted friends told him it was the right thing to do. But the mere thought of his beloved wife pumped with drugs in an environment that was not home was enough for him to reconsider.

It became clear that McQuilkin could no longer be both the full-time president of the school and the full-time husband to his Muriel. He said of his decision, "When the time came, the decision was firm. It took no great calculation. It was a matter of integrity. Had I not promised, 42 years before, 'in sickness and in health . . . till death do us part'?"[2]

When he told the board he was resigning, McQuilkin was surprised by the lack of support he received from some. In fact, one person tried to talk him out of it. "She doesn't even know who you are," he said. McQuilkin's response: "But I do and I know what I must do."[3]

This man understood fully and committed to the vows he made when he married Muriel. He was steadfast even when it was hard, when he had to make sacrifices, when he had to act selflessly. How many of us can say the same about our level of commitment?

### Step 3: Be Aware of Your Greatest Temptation

There are times in your life when someone hurts you and your pain is so great you may feel justified in doing the wrong thing. You may feel justified in not forgiving a spouse who has cheated on you. You may feel justified in walking away from a family member who has deeply disappointed you. You may even feel justified in seeking revenge.

> We are most vulnerable to temptation, to doing the wrong thing, when we can justify it the best.

I believe we are most vulnerable to temptation, to doing the wrong thing, when we can justify it the best.

Most people think the greatest temptation Jesus ever faced was when Satan approached Him after His forty-day fast in the wilderness. I believe it happened just before He was crucified.

When Jesus was praying in the Garden of Gethsemane, He knew that in only a few hours He would be beaten, tortured and hung naked on a cross. He was in anguish as He prayed, sweating drops of blood. "My Father! If it is possible, let this cup of suffering be taken away from me. Yet I want your will to be done, not mine" (Matthew 26:39).

After He prayed, Roman soldiers swarmed the Garden and arrested Him. Trying to defend Jesus, an enraged Peter cut off the ear of one of the assembled men. Jesus turned to Peter and said,

Put away your sword. Those who use the sword will die by the sword. Don't you realize that I could ask my Father for thousands of angels to protect us, and he would send them instantly? But if I did, how would the Scriptures be fulfilled that describe what must happen now?

Verses 52–54

Jesus had the ability to end this! He could have come up with plenty of reasons not to follow through with God's plan. And, frankly, no one would have blamed Him!

This was His greatest temptation.

The times you are tested the most are when you can justify being ugly, vindictive or outright mean. You can justify, as they say, "giving it to people as good as they gave it to you." You can justify feeling sorry for yourself because someone you loved betrayed you.

Your greatest temptation will come with your greatest justification. But what you do not see is that the greater the temptation and the greater the justification, the greater the manifestation of God in your life if you do not yield to that temptation.

> The greater the temptation and the greater the justification, the greater the manifestation of God in your life if you do not yield to that temptation.

I have said before that the ones closest to you can hurt you the most. When someone you love wrongs you or breaks your heart, watch your reaction. Resist the urge to get back at him or her. Forgive. If you need to, set boundaries. But you must forgive.

### Step 4: Say "I'm Sorry"—and Mean It

I have talked a lot about the importance and power of forgiveness when we have been hurt. I want to address the need for saying "I'm sorry" when we are the ones who hurt others, whether we meant to or not.

If you want to reconcile a relationship, you must be willing to say, "I'm sorry I hurt your feelings." "I'm sorry I said those things." "I'm sorry I didn't trust you." "I'm sorry I got so angry."

Here is another thought: Never ruin an apology by offering excuses. Never say, "I'm sorry, but . . ." Apologize and mean it.

We have all made mistakes and choices that we wish we could take back. But we can only move forward. Before you can truly move forward, you must humble yourself and repent. If the Holy Spirit prompts you to apologize, you certainly should. We are human. And we hurt others sometimes intentionally and sometimes unintentionally. Asking for forgiveness could be key in moving forward.

## How to Build a Successful Family

No matter how broken your family may be or how challenging a time you are going through, I am sure of one thing: You want your family to succeed. I am not talking in material terms, such as being the wealthiest family on the block. I am talking about building a family that serves God, in which every individual walks in his or her unique anointing and purpose.

Many families fail because we have learned how to have church at church, and when we come home we leave God at church. All we have in our home is a home. If we want to build and rebuild our families in the times that we are living in, we have to put church back in the home.

This requires balance. You cannot be so spiritual that you neglect natural things. And you cannot be so natural that you neglect the spiritual things. God's will is somewhere between Martha's kitchen and Mary's altar.

> You cannot be so spiritual that you neglect natural things. And you cannot be so natural that you neglect the spiritual things.

When Jesus came to Martha's house, all she cared about was the food on the table and how clean her house was. Everything needed to be in order. Mary, on the other hand, did not concern herself with these things. Rather than setting the table, she got down on her knees, poured oil on Jesus' feet and worshiped Him. We need both the spiritual and natural under the same roof.

Here are some things that I have learned from being married for thirty years (at the time of this writing) and parenting five children. I know it is the heart cry of every one of you parents to see your family succeed.

1. *Openly communicate with and express love to your spouse.* God knows that as parents we make mistakes. But we cannot do enough to mess our kids up if our kids know that their mom and dad love each other and are committed to one another.

   Children need to hear Daddy tell Mommy that he loves her. They need to see us touch one another. They need to see us hug one another. They need to see us walk through the mall holding hands. They need to see us enjoying each other's company.

   They will act like this affection is the grossest thing in the world, of course, but this is what helps keep a marriage strong. Families that do not do it are families that fail.

2. *Openly communicate with and express love to your children.* Kids need to hear from their parents, "I love you." They want Mom to affirm them. They want Dad to put his arm around them. If they do not get affirmation from you, they are going to get it from someone else! Families that succeed have parents who are affectionate with their children in a respectful manner.

3. *Enable open communication and expression of love between siblings.* I know this can be quite the challenge. I remember when most of my kids were teenagers at the same time. It

seemed someone was always fighting with another, and I felt like a referee! The Bible tells us not to let the sun go down on our anger (see Ephesians 4:26). Whenever our kids fought with one another, Cherise and I would make them talk it out and, importantly, hug it out. Half the time, it would be a begrudging, half–side hug, but soon enough, our kids would be back to loving on each other.

4. *Respect the personhood of each individual.* You might have different ideas, opinions or beliefs. Do not fight about your differences. While you do not necessarily have to agree with them, respect your family members.

5. *Respect personal property.* Your stuff is an extension of your person. We need to teach in our homes that you do not just walk in and steal your sister's newly purchased T-shirt and initiate World War III. You respect her property. Ask before you borrow.

6. *Respect their privacy, but consider their safety and well-being first.* It is a good idea to never enter a teenager's bedroom without knocking first. That said, you also have a responsibility to safeguard your children and reinforce established boundaries. I often hear parents say, "I respect my kids and give them privacy." I like to say, "You get privacy when you pay the mortgage." One time, after one of our daughters slammed her bedroom door in defiance one too many times, Cherise and I took the door off its hinges. It lay in the hallway for a month. Balance is key. In our home, Cherise and I will always have total access to everything, including each other's passwords.

7. *Establish, communicate and enforce boundaries.* We need to teach our children what boundaries are. I have talked about this throughout this book. What is the standard in your home? What are your boundaries? What rules have you set in place for your children and even for yourself?

Your kids may not like the boundaries you set, but you are responsible for enforcing them. You are responsible for the atmosphere in your home. You can have a yelling home in which the only time anybody does what you say is when you yell, or you can have a quiet home in which your kids listen with respect.

When you set boundaries and enforce discipline in your home, both parents must be unified. Kids will work their mom against their dad. They will mess you up as parents and get you arguing with one another. Set the stage for what will and what will not be tolerated. And be sure both you and your spouse are on the same page.

8. *Be committed to the process.* Just because one of your kids, say, your son, is freaking out and messing up right now, know he is not going to be like that the rest of his life. For instance, telling a lie is not the same as being a liar. Be patient and let the Lord complete His work in him.

9. *Place Jesus above all else.* Make Him present at all times, even in the little things. Acknowledge Him in every meal, through grateful attitudes, through reading the Bible together and praying as a family.

10. *Lead by example.* We teach through what our kids see us do in real life. My kids learn about forgiveness when they see me mess up and ask for forgiveness. Do not just preach to them; live out what you say.

## Create a Legacy

Every family, including yours, has a history rich in achievement. You may not know it, but in your family genes lie strengths that are unique and distinctive. To honor your family's past, you do not have to erect a monument. The greatest tribute you can pay is to remember lovingly the contributions and standards of the ones who have gone to be with the Lord and then to continue in their ways.

A wonderful way to build your children's self-esteem is to tell them about the great things God has done in their heritage. Tell them stories of God's faithfulness. Tell them about the miracles that have taken place. Challenge them to live up to the standards set by those who came before.

We hear a lot these days about generational curses. I think it is time we started passing on generational blessings to our children. They are transferable!

Jacob passed them on to his children, and you can pass them on to yours. Genesis 48:9 tells us that when Joseph presented his two sons born in Egypt to Jacob, Jacob said, "Bring them closer to me, so I can bless them."

> It is time we started passing on generational blessings to our children.

You do not need one million dollars or an impressive list of accomplishments in order to bestow an inheritance and blessing on your children. Just give them the values, the wisdom and the love that got you where you are. Give them the recipe for life that served your family well, and then challenge them to pass it on to the next generation.

Remember how my wife and I laid a Bible in the foundation of the house we built? You can do the same thing. Lay God's Word as your foundation. It is not too late to build your family. Even though your physical house may be built, today you are building your spiritual house.

## THE BIG IDEA

Build up the spiritual home of your family.

# CHAPTER ELEVEN

# FIGHT FOR YOUR FAMILY

During World War II, Adolph Hitler, who once dreamed of being a great artist, led the Nazis in the largest art heist in history. German forces plundered thousands of paintings, sculptures, artifacts and relics. Hitler's plan was to house these treasures for himself in a massive and beautiful museum he would one day build.

Had it not been for a group of Allied forces called the Monuments Men, many of these prized possessions of European culture would have been lost with the demise of the Third Reich. Organized as an Allied military unit during the war, this band of about 350 male and female art historians, museum curators and professors searched out the stolen loot. By the time the war had ended, the Monuments Men had helped track down (and eventually return) about five million cultural and artistic objects. In doing so, they helped preserve European culture for generations to come.

In the early stages of their salvage expedition, the Monuments Men were given little to no respect by combat soldiers; yet these men and women fought hard. One man in the task force, Second

Lieutenant Rorimer, had incredible resolve. I read how he once stood in front of a chateau that was on the list of protected monuments. The building had been set on fire and three of its four walls knocked down. This monument was barely standing.

It was not much more than a pile of rubble. But it was worth fighting for.

Rorimer heard the rumble of an approaching bulldozer. The massive machine thundered its way toward the protected monument on a demolition mission. As it got closer, Rorimer jumped in front of the bulldozer and boldly thrust out his hand, demanding that the driver stop.

A nearby commanding officer rushed over and insisted to the Monuments Man that he had no authority to tell anyone what to do. In essence the officer argued, "This is stupid. You're wasting your time. There's nothing here but a wall."

Rorimer had no intention of backing down. Informing the officer that he had taken a photograph of what remained of the historical building, he held up President Eisenhower's proclamation on monuments and war. "Do you want to spend the rest of your tour explaining why this demolition was a military necessity, not a convenience?"[1]

The officer in charge relented. And though ravaged by war, broken and ruined, what was left of this chateau was saved.

## Monuments Men and Women

I want you to think of yourself as a Monuments Man or Woman.

You have been given valuable treasures to protect. Your marriage is a valuable treasure. Your children are valuable treasures. Your loved ones are valuable treasures. And God has tasked you with fighting for them.

The bulldozers of hell are coming. They are rumbling toward you to topple the broken walls of your family. You can either let the enemy wipe them off the face of the earth, or you can stand in front of the ones you love and say, "In Jesus' name, I'm going to fight for my family!"

> **Think of yourself as a Monuments Man or Woman.**

Don't let hell take your treasures.

Your family might be a mess right now, but God can rebuild what has been broken or destroyed. If you choose to fight for your family, God will give you the victory.

## Get Your Fight On

If you want to love like you've never been hurt, you are going to have to start fighting for your family.

I am reminded of when God told Nehemiah—at the time a high-ranking official in a foreign country—to return to his homeland and rebuild the walls of Jerusalem. The city was a mess, in ruins from countless battles to destroy her.

Nehemiah gathered together the leadership of Israel and set to work.

> So I placed armed guards behind the lowest parts of the wall in the exposed areas. I stationed the people to stand guard by families, armed with swords, spears, and bows. Then as I looked over the situation, I called together the nobles and the rest of the people and said to them, "Don't be afraid of the enemy! Remember the Lord, who is great and glorious, and fight for your brothers, your sons, your daughters, your wives, and your homes!"
>
> Nehemiah 4:13–14

Enemies were coming to destroy the Israelites' homes, their marriages and their families. But Nehemiah was not afraid. He told the people, "Do not fear. Remember the Lord who is great and awesome!"

He told the people to fight.

"Fight for your sons."
"Fight for your daughters."
"Fight for your wives."
"Fight for your homes."
"Fight for your families."

It is obvious that the attack of Satan in the 21st century is on the home. The values that we cherish and the godly principles that we have dedicated ourselves to are worth fighting for.

If we want to win our families to God, we must do just one thing: fight for them! "The LORD will fight for you, and you shall hold your peace" (Exodus 14:14 NKJV).

I love the picture the Bible paints of Nehemiah's construction project:

When our enemies heard that we knew of their plans and that God had frustrated them, we all returned to our work on the wall. But from then on, only half my men worked while the other half stood guard with spears, shields, bows, and coats of mail. The leaders stationed themselves behind the people of Judah who were building the wall. The laborers carried on their work with one hand supporting their load and one hand holding a weapon. All the builders had a sword belted to their side.

Nehemiah 4:15–18

These men were building and battling at the same time. They had a tool in one hand and a weapon in the other. We live in a time when we must build up our family with one hand and fight the enemy with our other hand.

When Nehemiah endeavored to rebuild walls that had been torn down, immediate opposition came against him.

Is your family under attack today? Maybe your teenager is not serving the Lord. Maybe someone in your family has an addiction. Maybe you have not spoken to a loved one in months or years. Maybe unforgiveness or bitterness is infecting your family.

Decide today that you are not going to let the enemy have your family. Determine to fight for it.

Don't be content to let hell take the treasure out of the ones you love. Preserve your family. Remind yourself of what is important. Take responsibility for your family. Determine not to let the battering rams of hell destroy you or the ones you love. Determine not to let them perish. Get a sword in one hand and say, "I'm going to rebuild and I'm going to fight until I get the victory in my own home."

Here is good news—great news, in fact. God will fight for you!

Nehemiah said, "The work is very spread out, and we are widely separated from each other along the wall. When you hear the blast of the trumpet, rush to wherever it is sounding. Then our God will fight for us!" (Nehemiah 4:19–20).

**God will fight for you!**

If you fight, God will fight.

God will fight for your wives, for your husbands, for your sons, for your daughters, for your homes. No weapon formed against you will prosper! (See Isaiah 54:17.)

If you are determined to keep your family together, to reconcile relationships that are broken, to love the way God loves you, you'd better start fighting.

## Battle Plan

If you are going to fight for your family, you are going to need a battle plan. Read on to learn four strategies for claiming your victory.

### Strategy 1: Strip the Streaks

When God promised the Israelites that one day they would conquer the land of Canaan, He also assured them they would live in homes that had already been built. Leviticus 14 offers some instructions God gave to Moses and Aaron about these homes. In essence, He told them, "Watch the walls" (see Leviticus 14:37–42).

Here's what that means: Some of the houses in this area had been infected by a plague of leprosy. Scholars believe this was a consequence of prevalent idolatry practiced by the original owners.

When the pagan nations heard of the Israelites' flight from Egypt and how God had miraculously helped them escape through the Red Sea, they got scared. They figured the people of Israel would eventually show up and conquer their lands, too. In hopes of protecting their most prized possessions, idols made of silver and gold, they buried these statues deep in the walls, under the floors and behind stones in their homes.

When move-in day for the Israelites rolled around, God warned the people to watch the walls. If reddish or greenish streaks appeared, it was a sign that the house was contaminated. This was not something you could just wash off with soap and water or bleach. This was a serious spiritual issue that needed to be taken care of through a spiritual means.

A priest would inspect the home and, if necessary, remove the affected stones and put new ones in their places. If the streaks started to spread throughout the house, the house had to be condemned. The King James translation refers to this anomaly as "fretting" leprosy (verse 44)—one could say "angry" leprosy. God did not want His children living in homes that were spiritually condemned.

Your first assignment in your battle plan is this: Take some time and assess the condition of your home. I am not talking about the faded carpet, the new deck or the peeling paint. I am talking about the spiritual condition of your home.

Is it steeped in bitterness? Rage? Lots of yelling and screaming? Slamming of doors? Constant bickering? If you said yes to any one of these, consider these to be streaks in your walls.

Look, no family is perfect. Stress, tension and conflict are common to all. Your family environment is not always going to be saturated with smiles, laughter and hugs from sunup to sundown.

The streaks God wants you to get rid of are the constant strife that is taking a toll on your relationships: the never-ending battle between you and your rebellious child; the weeks that pass in which you and your spouse barely speak a word to each other; the unwarranted accusations that fly out of your mouth and forge another crack in your already-broken relationship.

If this sounds overwhelming, be encouraged. Jesus can clean your house. But first, you have some stripping to do.

> Take some time and assess the spiritual condition of your home.

If you are going to be victorious in the fight for your family, it is time to take responsibility. Think about these questions: Have you compromised your activities? Have you compromised in whom you hang out with? Have work, going out after work or video games become more important than spending time with God? Are you having conversations with friends that often turn into gossip fests? Do you tolerate rebellion? Is discipline nonexistent in your home? Do you allow your kids to go to this party or that sleepover without verifying where they are or that a parent is present? Are you searching things on the internet that you know you shouldn't? Or watching pay-per-view features you have no right watching? Are you speaking blessings or curses over your family? Do addictions fester in your home? Do you wrestle with unforgiveness? Does alcohol or any other substance—illegal, prescription or otherwise—have power over you?

Strip the streaks. Set a right standard in your home. Get rid of filth and foul talk. Be watchful of what is going on with your kids. Allow God to cleanse your spirit and set you free. Allow Him to remove the bitterness and replace it with joy. Allow Him to remove the anger and replace it with peace. Allow Him to remove the contempt and replace it with love.

God can take a family torn apart and put it back together again. After you meditate on the self-inventory questions I asked above and spend time in prayer asking God to renew a right spirit within you, follow these three steps to start stripping the streaks from your house:

1. *Anoint your house.* When you anoint your home and your family, you are telling the Holy Spirit He is welcome.

2. *Speak a blessing over your home.* This is a command. Here is a good one: "May the LORD bless you and protect you. May the LORD smile on you and be gracious to you. May the LORD show you his favor and give you his peace" (Numbers 6:24–26).

3. *Serve communion in your home.* My longtime friend Perry Stone wrote a book called *The Meal that Heals.* This is what communion does: It heals! It is almost impossible to fuss and argue if you know you are going to come together as a family and share communion.

### Strategy 2: Commit to Your Commitments

If you want peace in your home, if you want a long-lasting marriage, if you want generations of family to continue to serve the Lord, commit your path to God.

Do not waver in your faith. Do not compromise your standards. Set the right priorities for you and for your loved ones.

Jeremiah 6:16 gives us some great advice: "Stop at the crossroads and look around. Ask for the old, godly way, and walk in it. Travel its path, and you will find rest for your souls."

Don't let culture define or influence your identity, your values or your family.

As you raise your family, settle in your heart that you and your loved ones will be committed to God. You will go to church together. You will read the Bible together. You will be a God-honoring family.

You might argue, fuss, get mad, pout, be sour or speak ugly to one another every once in a while, but when all is said and done, determine to be committed to God. Remember who is on your side, fighting for you! And always be quick to forgive.

Most of us know David as a man after God's own heart (see Acts 13:22). God had plenty of great things to say about this man—though he was not a perfect man, nor did he always get his priorities straight.

In fact, we read in 1 Kings 15:15 that "David did what was right in the eyes of the LORD, and had not turned aside from anything that He commanded him all the days of his life, *except in the matter of Uriah the Hittite*" (NKJV, emphasis mine).

> Don't let culture define or influence your identity, your values or your family.

Uriah was one of David's warriors. He was even listed, as I wrote before, in the genealogy of Jesus as the husband of Bathsheba. David, the man after God's own heart, not only had an affair with Uriah's wife, Bathsheba, he also schemed to have Uriah killed to clean up his own mess.

There was something about Uriah that God got hung up on and could not look over. He impressed God. When I started studying this man, I observed that Uriah had a spirit of loyalty. I believe this is why God kept mentioning him over and over. Loyalty—or commitment—is a powerful concept. We, too, impress God when we are committed to Him, to the Church, to our marriages and to our homes.

You probably know that David had an affair with Bathsheba. (You can read the account of it in 2 Samuel 11.) She got pregnant from this encounter. Immediately, David devised a solution to the mess: He was going to cover up what he had done.

He sent for Uriah, who was on the battlefield.

"You've fought well for me," David told Uriah. "Why don't you take a break? Go home and be with your wife." David thought he had everything figured out. But he did not realize Uriah was a man of loyalty.

Uriah did not go home. He felt convicted because his fellow comrades were out fighting on the front lines and he was not with them. So he slept by the door of the palace with the king's servants.

The king tried again. The next night David got the man drunk, hoping the booze would make him feel all lovey-dovey and prod him to go home and sleep with his wife. But that didn't happen, either. Funny, Uriah had more conviction when he was drunk than most people do sober. How do you explain that? The spirit of loyalty. Uriah was a committed man.

He was loyal on the battlefield. He was loyal in his home. He was loyal in his convictions to God. David, on the other hand, was still trying to weasel his way out of his sin. Faced with the prospect of his sin being exposed, he decided he had no other option but to have Uriah killed. He sent the man back into the throes of battle, assigning him the task of carrying a letter to the commanding officer. Uriah had no clue that he was holding in his hand his own death warrant. In the document, David demanded that Uriah be sent to the front lines so "he may be struck down and die" (2 Samuel 11:15 NKJV).

And that is exactly what happened.

You may find yourself in a situation you ought not to be in, but if you have enough of God's Word in you, you won't sin. Proverbs 11:3 (NKJV) says, "The integrity of the upright will guide them." And in Psalm 119:11 (NKJV), we read, "Your word I have hidden in my heart, that I might not sin against You."

When family life gets tough, a temptation will come to quit, to stray or to compromise. Maybe you are tired of fighting with your kids or with your spouse. Maybe you are in a tight financial spot. Maybe job stress is weighing you down. There's something to be said about being loyal in tough times.

Commit to the promises you made to your family. Strive to be faithful in all areas of your life. Shun the seducer. Resist the home-wrecking spirit. Remember the marriage covenant you made. Do not play with flirty text messages. Run away from temptation. Do not go places you shouldn't. Invest in your family. Play with your children. Get involved in your kids' lives. Take your son to the ball game. Take your daughter shopping. Say and do things that will bring honor to your family.

Thomas Carlyle wrote something profoundly true: "Conviction . . . is worthless till it convert itself into conduct."[2] Want to know the depth of your character? Follow through with the commitments you have already made.

Don't just talk about it. Do it.

### Strategy 3: Live by Your Convictions

One man in the Bible cracked the code on how to perpetuate faith through multiple generations of family. He was a man with convictions. More than that, he lived them.

Jonadab is first mentioned in 2 Kings 10, where he is referred to by the name Jehonadab. He became the right-hand man to Jehu, a man tasked by Elisha to take over the throne of Israel and wipe out idolatry in the nation, reinstituting the worship of the one and only God.

Jonadab was perfect for the job, for he had great zeal for the holiness of God. He opposed the religion of the day and refused to let idolatry seep into his family life. Jonadab was not interested in just playing church; his actions reflected his convictions.

Jonadab knew how powerful secular ideologies were, so he intentionally structured his family life around his relationship with God, not the whims or fleeting desires of culture. He determined not to allow spiritual compromise to enter his home. To this end, Jonadab set some rules in place: He did not permit anyone in his household to drink alcohol. This was not a mandate ordered by God, but Jonadab was a wise man. He knew that excess drink can often be a portal for foolish behavior and even sin.

Fast-forward 240 years and we find the depth of this father's influence. His convictions extended for at least six generations, for we read about his line of children in Jeremiah 35. Don't let the complicated names in this passage trip you up; stay with me.

> The word which came to Jeremiah from the LORD in the days of Jehoiakim the son of Josiah, king of Judah, saying, "Go to the house of the Rechabites, speak to them, and bring them into the house of the LORD, into one of the chambers, and give them wine to drink." Then I took Jaazaniah the son of Jeremiah, the son of Habazziniah, his brothers and all his sons, and the whole house of the Rechabites, and I brought them into the house of the LORD, into the chamber of the sons of Hanan the son of Igdaliah, a man of God, which was by the chamber of the princes, above the chamber of Maaseiah the son of Shallum, the keeper of the door. Then I set before the sons of the house of the Rechabites bowls full of wine, and cups; and I said to them, "Drink wine."
>
> But they said, "We will drink no wine, for Jonadab the son of Rechab, our father, commanded us, saying, 'You shall drink no wine, you nor your sons, forever. You shall not build a house, sow seed, plant a vineyard, nor have any of these; but all your days you shall dwell in tents, that you may live many days in the land where you are sojourners.' Thus we have obeyed the voice of Jonadab the son of Rechab, our father, in all that he charged us, to drink no wine all our days, we, our wives, our sons, or our daughters, nor to build ourselves houses to dwell in; nor do we have vineyard,

field, or seed. But we have dwelt in tents, and have obeyed and done according to all that Jonadab our father commanded us."

Jeremiah 35:1–10 NKJV

For six generations, the men in Jonadab's family had kept the convictions their great-great-great-great grandfather had put in place for his household. Isn't this amazing? Jonadab set a godly standard for his family. It was not the standard of his neighbor. It was not the standard of the father down the street. It was certainly not Hollywood's standard. He set apart his family for God, and 240 years later, his offspring were living by those very same principles.

We must identify things in our lives and in our families that do not glorify God, and then we must boldly remove them from our homes. Not for the sake of following a set of rules, but to fiercely protect those we love.

This is how we create a spiritual heritage. This is how we pass down the garment of faith. It takes strong mothers. It takes strong fathers. It takes courageous men and women who are willing to say yes to God and consecrate themselves, their families and their homes.

I admit that though I strive to be a good father, I have at times failed. I have made mistakes. I have spoken words I regretted. But I kept trying. And I still do today. I might fall tomorrow, but I'll get back up. I am going to keep standing because I choose to battle for the futures of my children, their children and future generations.

We all need to do a better job of saying no. Say no to drinking. Say no to popping pills. Say no to watching certain movies. Say no to having "harmless" lunches with colleagues of the opposite sex. Say no to gossip and all forms of lewd speech. Say no to letting your children hang out with whomever they want and go wherever they please.

The coolest thing about Jonadab's life is what God promised because he stuck to his convictions. God said, "Jonadab the son of Rechab shall not lack a man to stand before Me forever" (Jeremiah 35:19 NKJV). In plain speak, "Every descendant of Jonadab will serve Me."

What a promise! What a God! No matter how society or culture changes with each generation, our heavenly Father can bless those who choose to set a standard in their homes and fight for the souls of future generations.

> **Inscribe the message of Joshua 24:15 upon your heart: "But as for me and my house, we will serve the LORD."**

Your home can be blessed. Your home can have peace. Your home can have joy. The favor of God can come upon your dwelling place. But you have to take whatever you know in your heart that God is not pleased with and throw it over the wall.

Live by your convictions. Refuse to compromise. Inscribe the message of Joshua 24:15 (NKJV) upon your heart: "But as for me and my house, we will serve the LORD."

### Strategy 4: Fight for What's Left

I wonder if you have suffered a loss. Maybe your husband just left you. Maybe one of your children passed away in a tragic drunk-driving accident. Maybe your teenager ran away. Maybe someone you love committed suicide. I want you to read the next few words carefully and slowly.

God is still the God of what's left.

You may not feel this to be true, but if you hold on to your faith, God is going to use the rubble, the tears and the heartache for a greater purpose.

Amos 3:12 (NKJV) paints a great picture, though when you first read it, it might seem strange: "As a shepherd takes from the mouth of a lion two legs or a piece of an ear, so shall the children of Israel be taken out who dwell in Samaria—in the corner of a bed and on the edge of a couch!"

A beautiful allegory is being painted in the first part of this passage. A lion had devoured a lamb. And the only thing left for the shepherd to salvage was two legs and a piece of an ear. It did not matter how broken the lamb was or that what was left seemed hardly worth the trouble; the shepherd fought for what was left. To him, the remains were significant. They mattered. They had purpose. They were worth redeeming.

If you are hurt, weighed down by trouble or struggling through family conflict, it is not over. You may not have what you used to have. Your life may look different. But you are not finished.

If you still have an ear to hear and a leg to stand on, you can stand on God's Word. You can find hope in the promise that "though your beginning was small, yet your latter end would increase abundantly" (Job 8:7 NKJV).

> If you still have an ear to hear and a leg to stand on, you can stand on God's Word.

When hell tries to decimate your relationships with your loved ones, it is easy to let the bulldozers come and topple the broken walls that are barely left standing. But remember, you are a Monuments Man. You are a Monuments Woman. You stand up and you fight for what is left.

You may look at your family today and see a war-ravaged home. Fight for what's left.

If you are still hurting from a divorce that you desperately tried to stop, fight for what's left.

If one of your children was killed in a horrible accident, fight for what's left.

If a senseless tragedy has tried to steal all hope in your heart, fight for what's left.

Did you know the walls Nehemiah built are still standing today? This is how important it is to fight for your family. Fight. Pray. Fast. And keep doing it. If you do not give up on your family,

**The miracle is not found in what was lost. The miracle is found in what you have left.**

your walls will stand for generations. Fight for what's left, and God will fight for you.

Talk again. Pray again. Try again. Forgive again. Reach out again. Go to dinner again. Refuse to give up. Refuse to allow depression and worry and anxiety and frustration to overcome. Fill your valley with prayer. Fill it with praise. Fill it with Scripture.

The miracle is not found in what was lost. The miracle is found in what you've got left.

## THE **BIG** IDEA

Fight for your family.

# CHAPTER TWELVE

# LOVE GOD LIKE YOU'VE NEVER BEEN HURT

When a co-worker who happened to be a Christian asked Wayne Caston out to lunch one day, it seemed to come out of the blue. What the man said to Wayne while they ate was even stranger.

"God spoke to me in my heart and told me to tell you, 'It's going to be okay.'"

Wayne wasn't sure what his co-worker meant by this. He just nodded and said, "Okay. Well, thanks for whatever that is."

A few weeks later, he understood.

On the morning of Easter Sunday in 2007, Wayne and his wife, Debbie, were getting their family ready for church. The Easter baskets had already been unwrapped, to the delight of Ross, eight, and Claire, eleven. For Charles, eighteen years old and a high school senior, it wasn't the chocolate bunnies and jelly beans that sparked his excitement. It was the brand-new golf putter that sat beside his basket. Planning on attending Young Harris College with an academic scholarship in the fall, Charles had been working on his swing in hopes of making the school's golf team. This putter was one he had always wanted.

Charles had just come home from spring break late the night before. "Stay home," his parents had told him early that morning. "You've been driving all night. You must be exhausted. Go back to bed and get some rest."

Charles laughed. "It's Easter! Of course I'm going with y'all to church."

Debbie took the wheel of the SUV that morning, and Claire hopped in the passenger seat. With a steaming hot mug of coffee balanced in his hand, Wayne climbed the foot pedestal into the back row next to Ross. Charles was the last to pile in, and Wayne decided to give up his window seat to his oldest son, squeezing in between his boys in the back.

Ten minutes into the drive to church, Debbie noticed a car barreling through a stop sign onto the highway, headed right toward them. She swerved immediately to avoid a collision, but the other car slammed at full speed into the passenger side of the Castons' vehicle. The SUV spun out of control and rolled several times until it came to a stop on the driver's side.

Upon impact, every family member except for Wayne and Charles was thrown out of the vehicle. Wayne remembers looking at his son, whose head now rested on the highway's asphalt, the window next to him having been shattered. Charles's eyes were closed and he was unresponsive. Wayne didn't see any blood on his head, and he hoped that was a good sign.

Numb from shock, Wayne managed to climb out of the mangled vehicle to look for his wife and two other children. He found Claire sitting beside the SUV. She was alive, but her left leg was degloved from her knee to her foot. "The entire inside of her leg was exposed," Wayne told me. "I could see blood, tissue, tendons, bones."

He found his wife lying down on the road, conscious but groaning in pain. Ross was farther away, his body sprawled out on the white line of the highway. He was bleeding, but nothing looked broken. "Are you okay, Ross?" Wayne asked, still in a daze. Ross managed a meager smile and replied, "Hey, Dad."

By the time Wayne returned to the vehicle to check back in with his oldest son, the accident scene was flooded with members from the Baptist church across the highway who had seen or heard the crash. First responders had also just arrived and began to work furiously on the victims. Wayne remembers a paramedic telling him at one point that Charles was alive, that he could detect a faint heartbeat. A few minutes later, he asked the same paramedic how his son was doing. This time, the young man said nothing. He just shook his head.

Wayne knew what that meant. Charles was dead.

"Knowing my son was gone," Wayne told me, "and seeing every other family member scattered on the highway somewhere, bleeding, I shut down. Everything went gray at that point. I just sat down on the ground and stared into the woods. I was more broken than I ever imagined was possible."

Ross and Claire were airlifted to Egleston Children's Hospital in Atlanta. Later, paramedics told Debbie and Wayne that none of them thought either child would survive. Ross's skull was cracked and his brain bleeding. Claire started to turn gray in the helicopter from a severe loss of blood. If—and that was a big *if*—she lived, a leg amputation seemed inevitable. In the hospital, the two siblings were assigned separate ICU rooms. Neither was expected to survive the night.

Debbie had a skull fracture and had slipped into a coma. Wayne, who suffered minor injuries in his head and back, was taken with her to the local hospital. Assessing her injuries, doctors gave Debbie a 50 percent chance of survival. Wayne remembers his parents-in-law arriving at the hospital and asking where Charles was.

"I said nothing," Wayne told me. "I knew where he was, but I couldn't say out loud that he was dead. I couldn't admit it to anyone yet. It still didn't seem real."

I will never forget walking into the emergency room with Cherise and asking Wayne how he was doing. He looked at us, heartbroken, face bruised and marred with blood. With tears streaming from his eyes, he quoted Job 1:21. "God gives and He takes away. Blessed be the name of the Lord."

On Tuesday, Debbie woke from her coma. Filled with indescribable sorrow upon hearing the news that her firstborn had been killed and her two other children were in another hospital fighting for their lives, she prayed for the first time in days. "It pained me that I couldn't pray while I was in the coma," she says. "But I was tremendously encouraged to hear that during that time the hallways were filled with men and women on their knees, praying for our family."

Doctors released her from the hospital on Friday so she could bury her son the following day. I remember officiating the funeral. Hundreds of young people came. Even through a horrible tragedy, many lives were touched by the Lord that day.

Wayne left the hospital on Wednesday to see Claire and Ross. Since he had been hospitalized also, it was the first chance he'd had to check on his children. Miraculously, the plastic surgeon who worked on Claire was able to save her leg. This amazing girl has had twelve surgeries to date, five in the first week alone to remove bits of grass, gravel and glass buried in her leg. It has been a difficult road to recovery. Though she almost died in the hospital and still deals with physical issues with the leg, she is alive and well.

Debbie says, "There is no deeper pain than losing a child. When I found out Charles was killed, it felt like the devil had stabbed me with a pitchfork and twisted it over and over in my heart. For a long time after the accident, I felt like life was moving on with everyone else, but I was stuck on a stationary bike, pedaling furiously and going nowhere."

Wayne told me something that will always stay with me: "One of the hardest things I remember was having to iron the clothes

Charles was going to be buried in. I just cried and cried while trying to get all the wrinkles out. I have always trusted God, but during this time the question 'Why?' occurred in my mind a lot. Why did God perform as many miracles as He did that day, like saving Claire's leg, and not save Charles? Why couldn't He perform just one more miracle?

"The truth is, we will never know why this terrible tragedy happened to us. We must trust God in His omniscience while we are on earth. Scripture tells us that the Lord will not give us more than we can bear, but I can say we were at the very edge with our toes hanging over it."

What has amazed me about the Caston family is that even through unspeakable tragedy, loss and heartbreak, they have clung to their faith. Their love for God was unshakeable. Debbie told me, "God never promised bad things wouldn't happen. But He did promise to walk with us through the tough times. Even though our lives have changed forever, God's love is forever. I draw strength from Him each day." She told me about a journal she kept during this time in which she wrote down examples of God's faithfulness. "The way He showered us with love, especially through other people praying for us, providing for our needs and encouraging us, was unreal."

Though it was a long and painful road to healing, Wayne learned to love and trust God through it all. "Our family has gone through and still goes through relentless suffering," he told me. "It seems like a constant uphill battle at times. Romans 8:28 [KJV] says, 'And we know that all things work together for good to them that love God, to them who are the called according to His purpose.' We find ourselves remembering that verse daily.

"Through this tragedy, my wife and I have grown closer to God. We've had to stay connected to Him. I don't think we had a choice. I can truly say that I trust God now more than I ever have. When things like this happen, you find out how delicate life is and how quickly things can change. Our time on earth is short. This is not our final destination. I know I will see Charles again. And I will be with him in heaven longer than I was with him down here on earth."

Miracles in their faith journey continued. Claire wrote the following beautiful words in her college application essay:

> Even though I continue to wear only pants in public, keeping my scars hidden in an attempt to avoid ridicule and confrontation, I know God spared my life for a greater purpose, and I am diligently working hard to fulfill my calling. I am recovering and starting over with a greater hope.

## Prodigal God

I think about what Wayne told me: "I have always trusted God, but during this time the question 'Why?' occurred in my mind a lot."

I have not walked in Wayne's shoes, but I understand his questioning. Not that my friend was angry at God, but honestly I wonder how anyone could not get mad at God in the midst of such a tragedy.

Sometimes it seems God is a prodigal God—when He doesn't do things or act the way we think He should. When we think about God, often we imagine Him always being encouraging and miraculous. But there are times in life when He acts totally out of character. Like when the miracle does not happen. Or when tragedy comes knocking on our doors. Or when He is silent.

The Christian walk is a marathon, not a hundred-yard dash. If you are in it for the long haul, you are going to go through seasons of discouragement and even despair.

So what then? Do we give up? Do we abandon our faith? Do we choose to believe there is no plan or purpose for our lives or the struggle we are going through?

Of course we don't. We love God like we've never been hurt.

The enemy's number-one goal is to get you mad at God. Don't. Trust God. Love like you've never been hurt. Joseph did. So did Jesus. Acts 14:22 tells us that "we must suffer many hardships to enter the Kingdom of God." You are not going to get to heaven without tribulation.

Sometimes life goes from bad to unbearable. We are already maxed out on stress when something else comes crashing down.

I have good news: When life goes from bad to unbearable, a miracle awaits.

See, our enemy has one flaw. He will not leave bad enough alone. Sometimes he keeps pushing and pushing so much that he pushes us straight into the arms of God. The devil is his own greatest enemy because he is constantly overplaying his hand. Sometimes we are so hard pressed that we finally realize we have to do something. We have to pray. We have to start going to church. We have to get counseling. We have to start loving God like we've never been hurt.

> The enemy's number-one goal is to get you mad at God. Don't. Trust God. Love like you've never been hurt.

God may not have been your first choice, but He has become your last chance.

Joseph had a dream from God that his brothers and parents were going to bow down to him. And then everything went backwards. He was abandoned by his brothers and he took a step backwards. He was sold into slavery and took another step backwards. He was falsely accused of rape and thrown into prison. More steps backwards. When he finally sat down, there was a throne under him.

You may be heartbroken by a loss or crisis in your family, but God is going to take you where He told you He was going to take you. It does not matter if you are moving forward in it or if you are reversing into it.

If your bad has become unbearable, it is time for good things to happen. It is time for deliverance. It is time for a miracle.

## Believe the Promise

When is the last time you cracked open a fortune cookie and read the message on the tiny slip of paper inside? You were probably encountering the work of Donald Lau, a successful—no joke—fortune cookie writer.

For thirty years Lau worked for Wonton Food Inc., the world's largest producer of fortune cookies. Lau wrote about two or three axioms a day. He strove to craft wisdom, inspiration and wit in a sentence of about ten words. That cannot be easy to do.

A former banker, Lau began working for Wonton Food in the 1980s. The role of fortune cookie writer fell into his lap because out of all the employees in the company, his English was the best. After creating a few fortunes a day for three decades, his creative processes began to slow down. Writer's block set in, and Lau was penning only two or three fortunes a month.

In 2016, Lau, who also serves as vice president and chief financial officer, stepped down from his role as fortune cookie writer. He hopes the legacy will continue and his mission to make customers "feel better" will continue through new generations.[1]

This man, who claims he is the most read author in the United States, said, "I don't think fortune cookies are meant to be like a horoscope. It's a way to end a meal in a Chinese restaurant and be happy when you leave."[2]

Have you ever heard someone say, "I want a word from the Lord"? Maybe you have said this yourself. The word we want to receive is usually something hopeful and encouraging—like a fortune you pull from a cookie.

"You will be blessed."

"Things will soon change for the better."

"You will find a large sum of money."

"Happiness will be yours."

What if you opened a fortune cookie and it said this instead?

"You'll still be single in another five years."
"You'll probably lose your job next month."
"Your husband will never come home."
"You are going to get sick."
"You will not get the promotion."

No one wants to hear messages like these. And yet, life is hard. We win, we lose. We love, we get hurt. We triumph, we fail. We do the right things and still experience struggle, loss, divorce, bankruptcy, abandonment, death and disappointment.

I do not know why bad things happen. God may not answer your why. Some of us may not know the purpose for our pain until we get to heaven.

Here's what I can tell you: When you are in crisis, God is not. When you are under another wave of depression, God is not. When you are lost in a valley and have no idea what to do, God has not vanished. He is still the healer. He is still the deliverer. And He is still working out a plan for your life.

> **When you are in crisis, God is not.**

Just because you may not understand the path you are traveling does not mean God isn't leading you. He may not give us answers, but He will always give us a promise.

Choose to trust Him. Choose to believe:

He will comfort you in all your troubles (Psalm 23:4).

God will meet all your needs (Philippians 4:19).

He will turn your darkness into light and make straight your crooked paths (Isaiah 42:16).

Joy comes in the morning (Psalm 30:5).

God will not forsake you (Psalm 9:10).

He will repay you for the years the enemy has destroyed (Joel 2:25). No weapon formed against you shall prosper (Isaiah 54:17).

And if I go and prepare a place for you, I will come again and receive you to Myself; that where I am, there you may be also.

John 14:3 NKJV

I don't know about you, but I take much more comfort and place much more faith in the promises of God than I do in the promises of government, the stock market, social media, doctors or so-called experts in any field.

When I look back, I see times when it seemed like everything worked perfectly and exceeded all my expectations. There were other times when nothing went right and I had to reach up while touching rock bottom.

No matter what storms come, the key is to continue to love and trust God. When you spend time in prayer and read His Word, you will be equipped to manage crisis and stand firm in troubled times. You will begin to love God like you've never been hurt.

Job had it right when catastrophe hit and he chose to believe, "Though He slay me, yet will I trust Him" (Job 13:15 NKJV).

## Teach the Angels a Thing or Two

Most of you know Job's story. At the whims of the devil, this man's wealth was destroyed, his children were killed, his reputation was smeared by his own friends and his wife pretty much gave up on him.

As doubts and questions weaved through immeasurable grief, Job had a decision to make: Curse God and die, or keep trusting Him.

Job chose to love God like he'd never been hurt. In essence, he said, "I don't have answers for what's happening to me, but I'm going to worship You anyway, because You're in control." Now, Job was not numb to the tragedies that befell him. Please understand that he struggled in the seeming absence of God. "I travel East looking for him—I find no one; then West, but not a trace; I go North, but he's hidden his tracks; then South, but not even a glimpse" (Job 23:8–9 MESSAGE).

Still, he worshiped: "But as for me, I know that my Redeemer lives" (Job 19:25).

Job could teach the angels a thing or two about worship.

Let me explain: Angels were programmed by God to worship. When Lucifer, the top dog of angels, turned his back on God and left the throne room of heaven, a third of the angels followed his lead. The angels that remained turned the volume up a notch and started praising God on a higher level. Like Job, they had a choice. They could have followed the enemy. Instead, they determined to serve God.

> **It is one thing to worship out of duty. It is another thing to choose to worship from a deep desire.**

Somehow I think their singing was even sweeter to the Creator. It is one thing to worship out of duty. It is another thing to choose to worship from a deep desire.

When the blood of Jesus cleanses us, the Bible says, the angels are being taught by us according to how we handle the crises and the trials, the good times and the bad times in our lives: "To the intent that now the manifold wisdom of God might be made known by the church to the principalities and powers in the heavenly places" (Ephesians 3:10 NKJV).

We are teaching the angels how to worship. We are teaching the angels the manifold wisdom of God.

Angels have never felt adversity in the human realm. They have never gone hungry. They have never been divorced. They have never struggled in their relationships. They have never lost a job.

While you and I worship in a fallen world, angels worship in a holy and perfect atmosphere. When we determine in times of trouble to praise God, we are teaching angels.

The Bible tells us that God inhabits the praises of His people (see Psalm 22:3). There is just something about the power of praise. When it looks like you are losing, praise the Lord. When you are in the valley, praise the Lord. When you don't know what you are going to do, praise the Lord. When you get weary, keep praising the Lord.

Want to love God like you've never been hurt? Start praising Him.

## Keep Leaning

I heard a story years ago.

A pastor of a little country church would conclude each service by asking one of the members of the church to stand up and pray the benediction. When he called on one particular farmer, the man always prayed the strangest thing: "Oh, Lord, prop us up on our leaning side." It did not matter what topic the pastor preached, the farmer's prayer was the same. Finally, the pastor got curious. "Why do you always pray that same thing?" he asked the farmer.

The man responded, "Well, sir, it's like this. I got an old barn out back. It's been there a long time. It's withstood a lot of weather, it's gone through a lot of storms and it's stood for many years. It's still standing. But one day I noticed it was leaning to one side a bit. So I went and got some pine poles and propped it up on its leaning side so it wouldn't fall.

"Then I got to thinking about how much I was like that old barn. I've been around a long time. I've withstood a lot of life's storms, and I've withstood a lot of bad weather in life. I've withstood a lot of hard times, and I'm still standing, too. But I find myself leaning to one side from time to time, so I like to ask the Lord to prop me up on my leaning side."

I figure a lot of us get to leaning at times. Sometimes we get to leaning toward anger, leaning toward bitterness, leaning toward hatred, leaning toward shame and condemnation, leaning toward a lot of things that we shouldn't. So we need to pray, "Lord, prop us up on our leaning side, so we will stand straight and tall again to glorify You."

> Lord, prop us up on our leaning side, so we will stand straight and tall again to glorify You.

If you have ever been in a hurricane, you know how powerful these storms are. Hurricanes can have a diameter of four or five hundred miles, wind speeds of up to two hundred miles per hour, storm surges higher than fifteen feet and rainfall up to forty inches. The damage that hurricanes inflict when reaching land can be astronomical. Trees are ripped out of the ground. Buildings are flattened. Entire towns are wiped out by floods.

Even more fascinating than the raw violence of hurricanes are two components of them—a hurricane's eye and the eye wall. The eye wall is an area of vertical clouds that surround the eye, which is the center of the storm. The eye wall is home to the most violent aspects of the hurricane—the most damaging winds and rainfall. In contrast, the eye of the hurricane is calm. Extending from twenty to forty miles, this area is mostly free of clouds.

See, God doesn't take away all our troubles—at least not as quickly as we would like Him to—but He promises us peace in the midst of them. He will prop you up. Sooner or later, you are going to feel the pounding forces of spiritual Mother Nature. And when these storms come, notice where you start leaning.

As you read this book, you might be leaning somewhere you shouldn't. It might have been a long time since you have felt God.

You might feel so overwhelmed by loss, pain or heartbreak that you are leaning not on Him but on an addiction, a weakness or unforgiveness. You might be hitting the bottle. You might be clicking on porn. You might be wallowing in bitterness. Wherever you lean that is not of God will lead your heart to harden.

God does not promise to take away our troubles or our problems. But He does promise us peace during them. Jesus can keep you from being swallowed up by the winds and rain and waves—but only if you let Him prop you up.

Jude 24 says, "Now all glory to God, who is able to keep you from falling away and will bring you with great joy into his glorious presence without a single fault."

God knows what you are facing. He knows what you are fearing. He knows what you are feeling. Whether you are battling cancer or depression or have lost a loved one, God will not let you fall to the darkness. When your marriage, your home or your family is leaning because of something that came at you like a hurricane, let God prop you up. God won't let you fall. This is how you love Him like you've never been hurt.

You may be leaning today, but you are not going to fall.

The winds are howling from house to house, from home to home, from family to family, from relationship to relationship. How are we going to make it? This verse in Song of Solomon gives me hope: "Who is this coming up from the wilderness, leaning upon her beloved?" (Song of Solomon 8:5 NKJV).

Are you in the wilderness? Lean on God, your beloved, and He will walk you out of that place. He will prop you up on your leaning side just as He did the Caston family. I read somewhere that 80 percent of couples divorce after the loss of a child. Debbie and Wayne are not part of that number. It has not been easy, but they have learned to lean on God while dealing with unspeakable pain.

Wayne told me, "We went through this tragedy together; why not see each other through it? It is easy to leave, but we made a commitment to God, and we intend to keep it. God performed many miracles that day, and if He will do that for us, He will do it for anybody. Not a day goes by that we don't think of Charles and what a blessing he was and is to our family."

## Three Encouraging Words

I do not know what you are going through today. Just know that you have come too far to collapse, fall, break down or give up.

I would like to encourage you with three truths:

1. You are doing better than you think.
2. You matter more than you think.
3. Don't give up on God, because He never gave up on you.

### *You are doing better than you think.*

You may have issues. You may have trouble reconciling with a loved one. You may struggle with unforgiveness. You may not be what or where you ought to be. But don't give up. You will get where God wants you by His grace.

You are doing better than you think you are.

Ecclesiastes 3 describes 28 times and seasons in life. There's a time to be born, a time to die, a time to laugh, a time to cry, a time to dance, a time to mourn and so on. The one time I don't see in this passage is the time to quit.

There is no time to quit in your life.

This week you may have gotten the worst diagnosis you could imagine. But you are reading this book for a reason. You want change. You want to love like you've never been hurt. Something in you is saying, *Even if I fall, I fall forward, and I'm going to go after God.*

You are doing better than you think you are.

### *You matter more than you think.*

It is easy to get discouraged when trouble comes and you are trying to do what is right. You may wonder what difference your efforts or your prayers make. Before you consider throwing in the towel, remember that you matter more than you think.

Imagine you hold in your hands a hundred-dollar bill issued by the United States Treasury. The Treasury has set the value of that bill at one hundred dollars. Let's say you buy some groceries with it. The bill finds its way into the hands of a corrupt person who bribes someone in a bad business deal; then it lands in the pocket of a drug dealer; then it makes its way into the cache of a prostitute. Finally, somehow, it finds its way back into your hands.

What is the value of the bill now? It is still one hundred dollars! A hundred-dollar bill's value does not change, no matter what it goes through, because its creator says that it is worth one hundred dollars.

> **No matter your pain, your loss or your sin, you are still what God created you to be.**

No matter your pain, your loss or your sin, you are still what God created you to be. You matter more than you think you do!

John the Baptist was a pioneer preacher. Before Jesus came on the scene, John told everyone that Jesus was coming. Later, he had the incredible opportunity to baptize Jesus and even hear the voice of God saying of Jesus, "This is My Son, with whom I am well pleased."

Years later, John found himself in prison, alone and very much discouraged. This man had paid a price to do what God called him to do, and in the process, he was rejected. People made fun of him. People called him crazy. Now he was in prison, waiting to be executed. Likely hoping for a word of encouragement from the man he had prophesied about, John sent for two disciples to relay a question to Jesus.

"Ask Him if He is the Messiah we've been expecting, or if we should look for someone else."

John's thought process sounds something like this: *I feel like such a loser! Have I been sacrificing and working and giving myself up to be mocked and tortured for nothing? I must not be doing everything right to get God's attention!*

Jesus' response to John's question is interesting. He gives John's disciples this reply: "Tell John about all the healings and the changed lives that are happening because of Me. And tell him not to be offended" (see Matthew 11:2–6).

I doubt these words brought John the encouragement he hoped for or expected. But the thing is, that's not all Jesus said. When the messengers left, Jesus turned to the crowd He was preaching to and said,

> What kind of man did you go into the wilderness to see? Was he a weak reed, swayed by every breath of wind? Or were you expecting to see a man dressed in expensive clothes? No, people with expensive clothes live in palaces. Were you looking for a prophet? Yes, and he is more than a prophet. John is the man to whom the Scriptures refer when they say, "Look, I am sending my messenger ahead of you, and he will prepare your way before you." I tell you the truth, of all who have ever lived, none is greater than John the Baptist.
>
> Matthew 11:7–11

*None is greater than John.*

The prophet never heard Jesus say these words! But they were still true. Jesus was saying, "John, if you could only see what I see, you would understand that you matter more than you think."

God says the same thing to you today. You matter. You are not a failure. You are not weak. You are not a loser. You are not insignificant.

You are important.

You matter more than you think.

**Don't give up on God, because He never gave up on you.**

Some time ago I married a family member of mine to a wonderful woman. This couple tried for years to have children but couldn't. Finally, they decided to adopt a child from China. They spent thousands of dollars and hundreds of hours buried in paperwork to make this happen.

The day finally came when, for the first time, they held that precious baby in their arms. I am sure that to that baby it was just another set of arms. But to that mom and dad, it was the greatest thing in the world. They cradled the child knowing firsthand the pain, tears and heartache of infertility. Holding that baby had more meaning than the little one would ever know.

It's less about you than you think.

I used to wonder why God did not just wipe out Adam and Eve when they sinned. Why didn't He start over? You know, try again.

Here is why: God is not in the business of replacing damaged people. God is in the business of fixing damaged people. He does not want to get rid of us. He wants to change us. He wants to heal us. He wants to transform us. He wants us to live out the message of the cross.

> God is not in the business of replacing damaged people. God is in the business of fixing damaged people.

A story is told about a man parked on the side of a road. His car had broken down, and he had the hood up, trying to figure out the problem. A limousine pulled up behind him, and a man got out. Dressed from head to toe like a million bucks, he walked over to the driver of the broken-down car and asked, "Do you need help?" The man, of course, said yes. The man from the limousine tinkered around with the engine a bit and, to the other man's surprise, the car started right up.

The car's owner was beyond grateful, and he asked how much he owed.

While there are many variations of this story, I heard one that included this response: "Nothing. I'm Henry Ford. I'm the creator of this car. It really bothers me to see one broken down on the side of the road, not doing what I created it to do."

God doesn't just ride by in His majesty and pass us along the side of the road when we have been broken. He wants to stop everything He is doing and come to our rescue. The Creator longs to redeem His creation.

It bothers God to see you not living the life He created you to live. He gets great joy when He sees you overcoming, when He sees you moving forward, when He sees your faith growing.

Do not give up on God, because He never gave up on you.

Trust Him today. Love Him like you've never been hurt. Whatever you are going through, whatever has happened, whatever loss or pain you feel in your heart, this is no time to quit. Be encouraged. If you continue to trust Him, God will not let you fall. He will not let you stumble. He will not let you wobble. He will walk you out of your desert standing tall.

## THE BIG IDEA

Love God like you've never been hurt.

# CHAPTER THIRTEEN

# KEEP CLIMBING

The enemy loves to use strongholds to keep us from the place God has called us to. The strongholds of unforgiveness, anger and bitterness are real. I want to teach you from the Old Testament how to defeat them.

A powerful moment in history and in Scripture is captured for us in the book of 2 Samuel. David led his men to what is now called Jerusalem to fight against its residents, the Jebusites. The Jebusites were tough, mighty warriors. And their city was set high on a mountain, a citadel that was surely fortified by impenetrable walls. Confident no enemy would ever successfully attack them, the Jebusites taunted David and his men. "You'll never get in here!" I can hear them mocking. "Might as well give up now!"

But David discovered their weakness: a water tunnel. He ordered his men to strike by climbing up this gutter and surprising the enemy on the other side. David's strategy was a success, and the fortress of Jerusalem was captured (see 2 Samuel 5:6–10).

The significance of this event is that it was the moment when the city of Jerusalem came to be. It was taken by the people of God and anointed for a prophetic purpose.

What is interesting is that right before this happened, the nation of Israel was split between those who followed David (the tribe of Judah) and those who recognized Saul's son Ishbosheth as king (the rest of the tribes). It was like a family war. Brother against brother. Kin against kin.

The tribe of Judah made the city of Hebron the capital. Though David was crowned king in Hebron, God had a greater purpose for him; He told David he was anointed to rule over the entire nation of Israel. He was destined to unite the family.

When the tribes came together and united under David's kingship, the time had come. I believe David sensed something in his heart—a deep desire to take over this impenetrable city. Positioned in the center of the former warring tribes, it was destined to be the capital city of the unified kingdom.

What strikes me about this story is how David could have settled. He could have been satisfied finally reigning over all of Israel in the city of Hebron. He could have sat back on his throne and taken a breather. But something in him called him to higher ground. A dream remained unfulfilled.

**Where you are is not your final destination.**

He could hear in his heart God saying, *Where you are is not your final destination.*

See, many years earlier, right after David had killed Goliath, he did something odd. He took the giant's head, dripping with blood, to the city of the Jebusites. I picture him sticking it on top of a spear and planting it right outside the walls on a hill.

I believe David was marking his territory—as if he were saying, "I'm planting this head here as notice that one day I'm going to come back and take this city for God, because God has given it to me. I have faith for it."

Years later, staring at the same walls of this impenetrable city, I think David must have recalled that stirring in his heart. He knew there was a place greater than where he was. He remembered and he moved out.

David and his men were destined to take over this city. It was not just something they wanted to do. It was an order straight from the throne of God. Some four hundred years after God commanded Israel to take over the entire land of Canaan, this was the only territory that remained unconquered. Even though it belonged to the people of Israel, to the untrained eye, it looked impermeable. Impossible.

**God is calling you to a place greater than where you are.**

God has not destined for your marriage or your family to be in conflict. He has not destined your relationships to be broken. He has destined you for reconciliation. God has destined you for victory over your marriage, over your family, over your relationships.

God's will is for your family to unite. He wants to break down walls that have caused division. He wants to reconcile differences. He wants you to love like you've never been hurt before.

God is calling you to a place greater than where you are.

## Calling Down All Strongholds

The Jebusites had set up a stronghold. And defeating them would not be easy. Throughout their history, the children of Israel had heard the legends of the Jebusites: They were mighty. They were fierce. They were powerful. A mystique surrounded them.

Knowing how fortified their city was, the Jebusites taunted David and his men. They were so confident in their stronghold, they teased the Israelites that even the blind and the lame could keep them out.

This is important, for it was a personal dig at two heroes of faith in Israel's history. The blind represented Isaac, who had lost his vision by the time he died. The lame represented Jacob, who after wrestling with an angel was injured and quite possibly limped for the rest of his life.

The Jebusites used psychological warfare against the Hebrew soldiers. "You don't belong up here. You're not powerful enough. You come from the lame and the blind. Be content with what you have. Settle for Hebron. Settle where you are and give up on the high place you are dreaming of."

Isn't the enemy great at flaunting our weaknesses right in our faces?

"You don't have what you think you have."

"Your father was a drunk. You will be one, too."

"This stronghold has been in your family for generations.
There's no way you can beat it."

David knew he had a fight on his hands. When you want to live God's best, when you desire a family who loves one another, stands with one another and is at peace with one another, you are going to have to fight to get there.

It seems we each have a natural tendency to want to fight. Put two little kids in an empty room, give them one toy, close the door and watch what happens. It will not take long for them to start battling it out.

But we are not children. As Christians living the Kingdom walk, we have to learn to fight right. Paul wrote, "We are human, but we don't wage war as humans do. We use God's mighty weapons, not worldly weapons, to knock down the strongholds of human reasoning and to destroy false arguments" (2 Corinthians 10:3–4).

I find it interesting that the pieces of armor God has given us, as found in Ephesians 6, are defensive. These include the breastplate of righteousness, the helmet of salvation and the shield of faith. The only offensive weapon in our spiritual arsenal is the sword of the Spirit, which is the Word of God. When you are battling for your future or the future of your family, the only offensive tactic you need is the Word. The Word will always be enough.

**Know what you are fighting for.**

When the enemy comes against you, he is after something. He does not just pick on you to pick on you; he is after the spoils. He is after you. He is after your spouse. He is after your children. He wants to take you and the ones you love and infect them with bitterness, unforgiveness, anger and offense.

Know what you are fighting for.

### The Dirtiest Battle = Your Greatest Victory

So David and his men stood before the mountain. A wide area on top had been flattened. Huge walls surrounded the city. There was no way in.

Then David's eyes fell on that weakness I mentioned at the beginning of this chapter: a water tunnel. This can also be described as a water shaft or a gutter. And David turned to his army and said, "First one who gets up the gutter . . ."

Have you ever cleaned out your gutters? It is an awful job. Once you pull on thick rubber gloves that reach to your elbows, it's time to start pulling out an endless pile of gunk and debris. Out come slime and sludge, twigs and leaves, remnants of bird nests and sometimes even small animals. It's just nasty.

That is what David was willing to climb through. He knew God had a bigger plan in mind. He knew God wanted him to do more than just settle for ruling in Hebron. God wanted him to take Jerusalem.

God said to David, "Hebron is what you can do, but Jerusalem is what only I can do. And I want you to get up there. It is not going to be easy. It is going to get ugly and dirty."

David had to climb the gutter. Victory comes in the strangest of places.

The first one up was a fighter by the name of Joab. He said, "Hold up—I've waited for this all of my life. Get behind me, young guns. I'm going up."

And Joab started climbing.

When he popped out the other side, you can imagine how much gunk and junk was splattered all over him. He looked bad. He smelled bad. But he raised his hands in victory and said, "God has given us this city!"

David and his men captured the city of the Jebusites. Wet, smelly and dirty, they conquered what rightfully belonged to them.

You may be facing a stronghold in your life. Maybe you are trying to save your marriage. Maybe you are trying to salvage a relationship with a wayward adult child. However big or intimidating the stronghold, God can set you free. He can raise your family up from the depths of bitterness, shame and unforgiveness.

> **The dirtiest battles of your life will produce the greatest victories.**

I do not know how dirty your battle has gotten. But I do know that it is the very place where God will be glorified the most in your life. It is where the anointing will come through. The dirtiest battles of your life will produce the greatest victories.

## Don't Settle

The fight for Jerusalem rages even in our lifetime.

At the turn of the twentieth century, Theodor Herzl, the visionary behind modern Zionism, embarked on a quest to establish a homeland for the Jewish people. At that point, they were scattered all over the world and had no place to call their own. In 1903, Herzl appealed to Great Britain for help. That same year, at the Sixth Zionist Congress in Switzerland, Herzl proposed the British

Uganda Program, developed through negotiations with the British. It called for the Jewish people to resettle on more than five thousand square miles in Uganda, Africa (now modern-day Kenya).

The idea was met with bitter controversy. Fierce and heated debates revealed widespread opposition to the plan. In fact, the proposition nearly split the young and passionate Zionist movement.

The British Uganda Program was plan B. Plan A was for the Jews to get their Holy Land back. Some believed they should just settle in Uganda and be content with what they could get. Maybe they would get their land later, but for now they should stick with plan B.

Others refused plan B outright. This was not what God had promised the people of Israel. They had a rightful claim to territory in Jerusalem and the surrounding areas. They should fight for their land.

Though the proposal was investigated briefly, the plan was voted down during the Seventh Zionist Congress in 1905. The majority of the delegates refused to consider any Jewish homeland other than the land of Israel, their Promised Land.

After the Uganda plan was rejected, Lord Arthur Balfour, a former prime minister of Great Britain, met with Chaim Weizmann, a Zionist in Britain who later became the first president of Israel. For Lord Balfour, the resistance of persecuted Jews to resettling in a safe area in Africa was inconceivable.

The story goes that Weizmann asked Balfour, "Suppose I were to offer you Paris instead of London."

"But, Dr. Weizmann, we have London," Balfour replied.

"That is true," Weizmann said, "but we had Jerusalem when London was a marsh."[1]

A man by the name of David Ben-Gurion, Israel's first prime minister, ultimately succeeded in establishing the independence of modern Israel. While the fight for Jerusalem is still ongoing, in 1948, the United Nations General Assembly, supported by the United States and the Soviet Union, agreed to the creation of the state of Israel. Ben-Gurion delivered the country's declaration of independence.

The enemy likes to offer us plan B. He wants us to settle. He wants us to stay in our places. He wants to keep us from dreaming big. He will give us all the reasons why we should not want more for our lives or for our families. He will show us why it is impossible to reconcile. He will try with all his might to extinguish the passionate fire for a place greater than where we are.

I wonder how many of you are settling for the Uganda plan in your lives. Maybe you have come to accept the fact that you and an adult child will never have a close relationship. Maybe you have come to terms with finally signing the divorce papers. Don't settle for the Uganda plan when God says, *You are headed to Jerusalem. I am going to give you the place of My glory.*

Don't settle for plan B when God says, "I am going to do exceedingly, abundantly above all that you can imagine" (see Ephesians 3:20).

Think about this: If David had settled for Hebron, God's plan for redemption would not have been carried out. Remember how David planted Goliath's head outside the walls of the city of the Jebusites? A thousand years later, Jesus was captured and brought into that same city. He was tortured and nailed to a cross at Golgotha, which is translated "place of the skull." Why was it called the place of the skull? Many scholars believe that it is the exact place where David put Goliath's head.

> I wonder how many of you are settling for the Uganda plan in your lives.

Genesis 3:15 (NIV) says, "And I will put enmity between you and the woman, and between your offspring and hers; he will crush your head, and you will strike his heel." When the Roman soldiers nailed the feet of Jesus on that cross, Satan bruised Jesus' heel. And with the thud of the cross driving into the earth, Jesus crushed the skull of Satan.

David's taking of the city of Jerusalem shows the plan of God. The enemy tried to thwart God's plan of salvation through a family squabble. When the tribes of Israel were divided, they would not have been able to capture the city of the Jebusites. The stronghold of that family had to be conquered so the power of the cross could be lifted.

Has the enemy divided your family and set up a stronghold? Through the power of the cross, you can take down strongholds. Through the power of the cross, you can defeat the enemy. Through the power of the cross, you can be victorious. God wants to give you victory in your place of the skull by renewing your thinking, something I talked a bit about in chapter 5. I'd like to share two principles for overcoming strongholds: Listen to what God is saying, and believe what God says is true.

### Listen to What God Is Saying

If you are in a fight for your family, don't let what you see hinder what God wants you to hear.

On a mid-October afternoon in 1982, sixty thousand–plus fans gathered to watch their football team, the University of Wisconsin Badgers, take on the Michigan State Spartans. Watching the game unfold on their home field, Badgers fans roared with anticipation of a win. Unfortunately, Wisconsin quickly began to trail the Spartans.

> If you are in a fight for your family, don't let what you see hinder what God wants you to hear.

Here's where the story gets strange. The further behind the Badgers fell, the louder the fans got. They shouted more. They clapped with more intensity. It made no sense. The Wisconsin teammates and coaches were stunned, listening to their fans scream with passion while they were losing badly.

Unbeknownst to the players on the field, many of the fans were listening to portable radios. About seventy miles away, the Milwaukee Brewers were beating the St. Louis Cardinals in Game 4 of the World Series.[2]

The people in the stands who were screaming louder with each passing minute were responding to what they heard, not what they saw. They were celebrating victory in the presence of what looked like defeat. What a picture of contradiction!

When David and his men stared at the city of the Jebusites, with their natural eyes they saw the rocky mountain, the impenetrable walls of the city and the mighty warriors that stood behind the walls. But they also heard the voice of the Lord, who promised victory in what seemed an impossible situation.

> **Are you responding to what you see or to what God says?**

Are you responding to what you see or to what God says? Think about it—really think about it. When you look at what lies around you, do you feel pressure? Do you feel overwhelmed? Do you feel fear? Defeat?

Scripture is clear that faith has nothing to do with what we see. We walk by faith, not by sight (see 2 Corinthians 5:7). Faith comes by hearing, not by seeing (see Romans 10:17). This is how we can be up in a down world.

Faith does not look at the facts and say, "Well, I might as well give up." Faith looks at circumstances that have "impossible" written all over them and then listens to what heaven is saying. And in heaven, you will never hear God say, "You should quit." "You're not going to make it." "Just quit already."

If you listen, you will hear God telling you that He is on your side, that He is fighting for you, that with Him you are more than a conqueror.

Determine today, as a person of faith, to move your eyes off your situation and open your ears to God's voice. Only then can you start moving toward victory.

Paul wrote,

> Therefore do not cast away your confidence, which has great re-
> ward. For you have need of endurance, so that after you have done
> the will of God, you may receive the promise: "For yet a little
> while, and He who is coming will come and will not tarry. Now
> the just shall live by faith; but if anyone draws back, My soul has
> no pleasure in him." *But we are not of those who draw back* to
> perdition, but of those who believe.

Hebrews 10:35–39 (NKJV, emphasis mine)

I love that phrase: *But we are not of those who draw back*. You
are not weak. You are not beat up. You are not defeated. You are
strong. You are mighty. You are a winner.

### Believe What God Says Is True

Second, believe what God says, not what you feel or what your
circumstances dictate.

In 1886, Walter George broke the one-mile world record when
he ran it in 4 minutes and 12.75 seconds. Nobody ran it faster for
thirty years. Then, in 1923, a Finnish athlete named Paavo Nurmi
shaved two seconds off the distance by running it in 4 minutes,
10.4 seconds.

That world record remained unbroken for eight years. After
that, the time kept getting shorter by a few seconds at a time, but
there was a widespread myth about not being able to break the
four-minute mark. Some doctors, in fact, were even reported as
saying it was physically impossible.

One man chose not to believe the lie.

In 1954, Roger Bannister broke the record for the first time in
human history when he ran a mile in 3 minutes, 59.4 seconds.
While I am sure there were plenty of athletes we do not hear about
today who believed it was possible to run a mile in less than four

minutes, it was Bannister who actually did. He defied the odds. He believed it could happen. And he worked and trained and practiced and sacrificed so he could be the one to break the record.

It's funny. This barrier has been broken many times since and is now the standard for middle-distance runners. What a powerful example of what happens when you get a new mindset.

If you have not figured this out yet, life is an uphill climb. On your way to the place, the purpose, the destiny or the high place that you are trying to reach in life, it is going to require some climbing. I found out in my own life that succeeding in marriage, family, relationships and my spiritual walk is an uphill climb.

God is looking for climbers. Climbers are dedicated. They face risks. They stare at mountains that look insurmountable. And they accept God's assignment to climb and conquer those mountains in His name.

Be encouraged and stay in the fight. Good news—God has already won!

## THE BIG IDEA

Don't settle. Keep climbing.

# CHAPTER FOURTEEN

# THE KING HAS ONE MORE MOVE

Marcus Luttrell was an elite Navy SEAL who survived a fierce battle in Afghanistan in 2005 and earned a Navy Cross for combat heroism. His bestselling memoir, *Lone Survivor*, documents his harrowing experience.

He and four other Navy SEALs were tasked with observing a village and capturing or killing a Taliban leader who had links to Osama bin Laden. While hiding out, this team noticed three shepherds. They thought about killing these men but opted not to.

A short time later, the team was surrounded by more than a hundred Taliban warriors. Luttrell writes that their decision not to pull the trigger on the shepherds may have signed their death warrant. A helicopter carrying sixteen special-operation soldiers about to rescue the encircled SEAL team was shot down; every single person on board was killed. Luttrell was the only survivor on his team. He was ultimately rescued by a group of Afghan villagers, who helped bring him to safety.

Early in the book, Luttrell narrates his experience working toward becoming a Navy SEAL, an elite soldier in the U.S. Navy's primary special-operations force. Many who attempt the more-than-yearlong period of vigorous formal training quit.

Early in their training, candidates go through what is known as "Hell Week." Hell Week is the defining week for these men. For five and a half days, they endure a continuous cycle of the hardest physical and mental exercises anywhere in the world.

Candidates are allowed at most only four hours of sleep during the entire week. During that time, they endure nonstop cold, wet and brutally difficult physical training. Hell Week is designed to weed out those who are not the best of the best. In fact, two-thirds of candidates do not make it.

During Hell Week, a bell is stationed outside the dining hall. When you feel the pressure is too great, the physical tasks too demanding, the fatigue too overwhelming, the muscles too sore, you can call it quits simply by ringing the bell. You don't have to explain yourself. Nobody will ask you questions. You ring the bell, go back to your barracks and eat a hot meal, and a bus will take you back to where you came from. If you want out of the Navy SEAL program, you can exercise your quit option.

In the book, Luttrell writes about watching strong, skilled candidates, one by one, quit and ring the bell. It was not because these men lacked physical strength or ability. They were some of the toughest men in the world. They lacked the mental fortitude to not give up.

One of Luttrell's instructors told him, "Marcus, the body can take . . . near anything. It's the mind that needs training. Can you handle such injustice? Can you cope with that kind of unfairness, that much of a setback? And still come back with your jaw set, still determined, swearing you will never quit? That's what we're looking for!"[1]

## Remove the Quit Option

When you have been praying for your family, for your marriage or for God to heal that broken relationship, there are times you may feel like giving up. Every single one of you reading this book has the option to quit. All you have to do is say, "I'm tired of the battle and I'm giving in."

I want to challenge you right now to remove the quit option from your life.

So do not throw away this confident trust in the Lord. Remember the great reward it brings you! Patient endurance is what you need now, so that you will continue to do God's will. Then you will receive all that he has promised. "For in just a little while, the Coming One will come and not delay. And my righteous ones will live by faith. But I will take no pleasure in anyone who turns away."

Hebrews 10:35–38

We need to understand that we are in a battle for our lives, a battle for our families, a battle for our marriages. The enemy is going to throw everything he can at us to discourage us. He is going to send strife, conflict, stress, contention, arguments and bitterness to try to make us quit.

But the battle is not what we see in the natural.

The battle is not about the trouble in your family. It is not about the financial problem. It is not about the sickness. It is not about the disagreements in your marriage. The enemy wants your mind. He wants to break you down mentally. He wants you to give up, to quit, to say, "I can't take this anymore!"

Marcus writes that while he was stunned to see some of the physically strongest candidates give up and ring the bell, he never once entertained the idea. The thought never even occurred to him.

The philosophy of the Navy SEALS is this: "I will never quit. . . . My nation expects me to be physically harder and mentally stronger than my enemies. If I get knocked down, I will get back up, every time. I will draw on every remaining ounce of strength to protect my teammates. . . . I am never out of the fight."[2]

Friend, your job is to not exercise the option to quit. Because when you make up your mind that you are not going to quit, that is when the battle is really won.

I have had prayers answered, and I have had prayers go unanswered. I have had miracles happen, and I have had huge disappointments. I have spent time on high mountains, where God gave me revelation and amused me in amazing ways, and I have spent time in deep, dark and low valleys, where it seemed God had forsaken me.

What I have learned through all this is that I'm never going to ring that bell.

I'm never going to walk away from God. I'm never going to quit my church. I'm never going to leave my wife. I'm never going to give up on my kids. I'm never going to let my dream die. I'm never going to quit preaching.

> **When you make up your mind that you are not going to quit, that is when the battle is really won.**

You have to determine the same thing. Lay hold of the truth deep down in your spirit that you are never going to quit.

If you are going to experience a successful marriage, you have to remove the quit option. You are going to need it when you aren't feeling wonderful and lovey-dovey. You are going to need the stick-to-itiveness when you do not feel happy. You are going to need it when your spouse does not thrill you the way he or she used to. You are going to need it when your kids are doing things that are contrary to what the Bible says and how you raised them.

A quit option is not built into a godly covenant marriage. It is for better and for worse. It is in sickness and in health. It is for richer or poorer. It is till death do you part.

I am enjoying the best time of my marriage right now. Cherise and I have been married thirty years. We have been through many ups and downs, but through the years, we hung in there. There comes a time in every marriage and family when it is easier to quit than it is to endure. But if you keep tapping, praying, forgiving and loving, you will enjoy a great reward.

## How to Survive Your Hell Week

Had Marcus Luttrell not endured Hell Week, he would not have survived the operation in Afghanistan in which all hell broke loose. When this man was surrounded by the Taliban, when he was the lone survivor in his squad, when he was wounded with a broken back and multiple fractures and when it seemed impossible for him to make it out alive, his mind was already made up. And he understood the vigor of his previous training.

So, how do you survive your Hell Week?

What do you do when the enemy throws your weakness in your face? What do you do when it seems every conversation with your spouse leads to an argument? What do you do when it seems you will never reconcile with your wayward child? What do you do when the pain of heartache is so great you feel that you cannot go on?

One, remember that the trying of your faith brings something more precious than gold. We read in 1 Peter 4:12–13,

Dear friends, don't be surprised at the fiery trials you are going through, as if something strange were happening to you. Instead, be very glad—for these trials make you partners with Christ in his suffering, so that you will have the wonderful joy of seeing his glory when it is revealed to all the world.

Two, consider Jesus. The book of Hebrews offers,

And let us run with endurance the race God has set before us. We do this by keeping our eyes on Jesus, the champion who initiates and perfects our faith. Because of the joy awaiting him, he endured the cross, disregarding its shame. Now he is seated in the place of honor beside God's throne. Think of all the hostility he endured from sinful people; then you won't become weary and give up.

Hebrews 12:1–3

Jesus endured Hell Week on the cross. He endured the accusations. He endured the ghastly torture. He endured the beatings. He endured the spit. He endured being stretched out on two pieces of wood. He endured the nails driven into His hands and His feet.

Jesus could have rung the bell. But He made up His mind in the Garden of Gethsemane that He was not going to quit. When He hung on the cross suspended between heaven and earth, He determined to do what God told Him to do.

If you are going through your Hell Week, consider Jesus.

Paul spoke of how he served God "with many tears" (Acts 20:19). He then said, "I don't know what awaits me, except that the Holy Spirit tells me in city after city that jail and suffering lie ahead" (verses 22–23). That's pretty sad! Nothing but trouble awaited the apostle in every city. But check out what Paul wrote next: "But my life is worth nothing to me unless I use it for finishing the work assigned me by the Lord Jesus—the work of telling others the Good News about the wonderful grace of God" (verse 24).

Paul was persecuted. He was beaten. He was stoned. He was put in prison. He was shipwrecked. He was judged. He was pressed beyond measure.

You would think at some point he would determine it was time to ring the bell. But here's the thing. Paul never said, "I've been through too much. I didn't sign up for this. God's given me more than my fair share. I think I'll just check out; it's time for me to give up. It's time to quit."

There was no quit in Paul.

Instead, he said, "I focus on this one thing: Forgetting the past and looking forward to what lies ahead, I press on to reach the end of the race and receive the heavenly prize for which God, through Christ Jesus, is calling us" (Philippians 3:13–14).

In other words, you cannot live in the past. The call is upward. You have to keep climbing. You have to keep moving. You have to keep pressing forward.

Don't give up.

As you read this book, you might be tempted to walk away from your marriage. You might feel like giving up on your family. You might see no possible way out of your battle. Be encouraged: Our God is a finisher. He who began a good work in you will be faithful to complete it! (See Philippians 1:6.)

> You cannot live in the past. The call is upward.

Don't quit. You belong in the high place, so don't settle for less than what God has promised you. If you will not quit, you cannot lose.

I want you to read the following statements below out loud. No matter what you are going through today, determine not to give up and to keep reaching forward:

I am never going to quit loving.

I am never going to quit serving.

I am never going to quit forgiving.

I am never going to quit praying.

I am never going to quit believing.

I am never going to quit being kind.

I am never going to quit serving God.

I am never going to quit loving like I've never been hurt.

## Checkmate

In 1831, a German artist named Moritz August Retzsch painted a fascinating work of art titled *Die Schachspieler*, "The Chess Players" (later called "Checkmate").

In this painting, two people compete in a game of chess. To the left sits Satan. He looks intimidating and wears a confident sneer. His opponent is a young man who stares at the board, perplexed. You can sense that this young man is in despair. He specifically stares at his king piece, which is nearly surrounded by his opponent's pieces. Checkmate. Game over.

I'm more of a checkers man than a chess man, but I do know how the game is played. The objective is to checkmate your opponent's king. When a king is surrounded, is unprotected or has nowhere else to go, that is a checkmate and the game is won.

Apparently, however, Satan's imminent victory over his rival is not all there is to the story. As one account has it, in the late 1800s, a famous chess player named Paul Morphy was visiting Richmond, Virginia. Word of his arrival circulated quickly. A prominent man in the community invited Morphy to his home for a game of chess.

During dinner, Morphy could not take his eyes off a painting in the room. It happened to be Retzsch's "Checkmate." The more he studied the work of art, the more interested he became. Finally, at the close of supper, Morphy walked over to the painting and examined it. Then he turned to his host and said, "I think that I can take the young man's game and win."

The host was skeptical. "Not even you, Mr. Morphy, can retrieve that game!"

"Suppose we try," challenged the chess champion.

Needless to say, the host whipped out a board and arranged it exactly as it was in the painting. To everyone's surprise, Morphy showed that the king had one more move. The young man in the painting was saved![3]

Does life have you in a checkmate? Do you feel trapped? Can't see a way out? Know this: The King always has one more move. Always.

Your spouse may give up on you, but the King has one more move. Your family may be experiencing more trouble than you can take, but the King has one more move. You may feel as if you will never have a happy home ever again, but I am here to tell you that the King has one more move.

God wants you to win. He wants you to go forward. He wants you to rebuild.

When your home is on the rocks, when the enemy whispers in your ear to walk away from your spouse and your kids, when your trials seem to scream "Checkmate," the King has one more move.

God's grace is enough. His love is enough. His anointing is enough.

Friend, your destiny is greater than your difficulty. Your destiny is greater than your disaster. Your destiny is greater than your present dilemma. Your destiny is greater than your fears.

> **Know this: The King always has one more move. Always.**

The King has one more move.

Proverbs 21:30 says, "No human wisdom or understanding or plan can stand against the LORD."

You don't have to be the brightest one on the block to know who is going to win the game of life, according to this Scripture. No knowledge, no power, no wisdom, no strategy and no counsel will come against God's purpose and plan and win.

This question remains for us: Whose side are you on?

Satan wants to checkmate our lives. The Bible tells us the enemy comes to steal, kill and destroy (see John 10:10). He wants to put us in a position from which we see no way out. He wants to steal our faith. He wants to steal our hope. He wants to steal our joy. He wants to steal our dreams. He wants to steal the promises of God from our hearts.

But heaven is fighting for you today.

You must get the revelation of Proverbs 21:30 deep into your spirit. Nothing is going to stand against God. There is no checkmate over your life. God is going to have the last move.

I think about the Israelites running away from Pharaoh and the land of Egypt. When Moses faced the Red Sea—with, according to ancient historians, mountains trapping them on both sides—Pharaoh's army was closing in, and fast. The Israelites were surrounded. There was nowhere to go. Moses and his people were surely going to die. And the enemy whispered in Moses' ear, *Checkmate. It's over.*

You must understand that God is never out of moves.

We say God can do anything, but that is not true. There is one thing that you and I can do that God cannot—we can reach the end of our resources. We can do everything we are able to do in some situations, but God has never done all that He can do.

You may have heard the doctor say, "Well, I've done all that I can do." Sometimes the counselor says, "I've done all for your family that I can do." But we serve a God who has never said, "I've done all that I can do."

> **Even when you feel as though you have given up on yourself, God will never give up on you.**

God has never done all that He can do. He always has one more move.

God will never give up on you. Even when you feel as though you have given up on yourself, God will never give up on you. God found Moses in his desert. God found Jeremiah in his pit. God found Joseph in his prison. God found Job in his tragedies. And God can find you.

Your job is to keep yourself in the love of God. To keep a good attitude. To keep your spirit lifted. To hold on to the promises of

God. And when you do this and the enemy whispers, *Checkmate,* your spirit will respond by saying, *I don't think so!*

## After This

Two words at the beginning of Job 42:16 have tremendous impact.

"*After this* Job lived one hundred and forty years, and saw his children and grandchildren for four generations" (NKJV, emphasis mine).

Job had gone through crises of catastrophic proportions. He lost his family, his health, his wealth. Everything.

But God gave him an "after this."

You may have lost a loved one. You may be dealing with a broken relationship. You may be wrestling with an addiction in your family, or you may even struggle with one yourself. God has an "after this" for you.

You are going to get through your struggle. You are going to live after your trial. You are going to live after your loss. You are going to live after your betrayal. The King has one more move.

> God has an "after this" for you.

Genesis 9:28 tells us that "Noah lived another 350 years after the great flood." He had more life to live after the flood.

There is life after the flood!

When God told Jonah to preach to the city of Nineveh, he said, "No way!" Why? Because he knew God would rather give the people forgiveness instead of judgment, and Jonah did not think they deserved that. So God made the first one-man submarine, a whale, and put Jonah in it. I will tell you this: You don't have problems until you have been sitting in the belly of a fish. But Jonah cried out for mercy. And God called out to the problem that had swallowed this man up and forced the whale to spit Jonah out. God is able to do anything. He always has one more move.

The soldiers who crucified Jesus thought it was over when He died. When, with blood-caked lips, Jesus said, "It is finished," and gave up His ghost, they put him in a tomb, sealed it and stationed armed guards to keep watch over it. One day went by. Nothing happened. Then two; still, nothing. Finally, three days passed, and Satan said, "Checkmate." But on that third day, when it looked like all was lost, Jesus rose from the dead.

> I believe you are reading this book today by divine appointment. God wants to tell you, "It isn't over."

The King had one more move.

Whatever you are dealing with in this very moment, know that God has one more move for you. It is a move of grace. It is a move of forgiveness. It is a move of mercy. It is a move of restoration. It is a move of miracles.

I believe you are reading this book today by divine appointment. God wants to tell you, "It isn't over."

## Key Principles Designed to Help You Love

It is my prayer that as you come to this final chapter, your faith has grown. You have a new understanding of the power of love, God's love. And you know how important it is to love like you've never been hurt.

Let's quickly recap what you have learned.

1. *God does His most stunning work where things seem hopeless.* Wherever there is pain, suffering and desperation, Jesus is there. The pain you feel today is the pain you can heal.
2. *Love never fails.* Choose love over hurt. Choose to love others—always. Choose to press forward. Choose to heal your wounds. Choose to keep driving.
3. *It is never wrong to love people who have messed up.* It is never out of order to love. You do not compromise your faith

when you love. This is what it means to love like you've never been hurt.

4. *It is unforgivable not to forgive.* Stop keeping score of offenses and start losing count.

5. *We can begin to love others when we love ourselves.* Jesus *commanded* us to love ourselves. As we do this, we become one step closer to the Kingdom of God, which is righteousness, peace and joy (see Romans 14:17).

6. *We are called to be kind.* It is not easy to be kind when the pressure is on, but that is what God calls us to do. Want to know how holy you are? Determine how kind you are.

7. *Instead of fanning the flames of discord, become a peacemaker.* We cannot position ourselves to love like we've never been hurt if we are ruled by our tempers. Internal peace affects the external atmosphere. Don't let strife infect you. Be a peace manufacturer.

8. *Marriage isn't just a good idea, it is God's idea.* Don't give up on your spouse. Don't give up on your marriage. God has big plans for you and the one you married! There is a door of hope in every valley of marital trouble.

9. *A committed and lasting marriage demands a made-up mind.* The enemy may have attacked your marriage, but perfect marriages do not make it to the cave of couples. The marriages that do have been through hell, but through the grace of God they have declared, "We will fight for what's left!"

10. *God is in the business of blessing families.* Nowhere else in this life will you find greater fulfillment and love than within the heart of your family. Don't give up on family. Go after them with the same love and grace and mercy with which God pursues you.

11. *Fight for your family.* Your family might be a mess right now, but God can rebuild what has been broken or destroyed. If you choose to fight for your family, God will fight for you.

12. *Love God like you've never been hurt.* Just because you may not understand the path you are traveling doesn't mean God is not leading you. He may not give you answers, but He will always give you a promise.

13. *Don't settle, and keep climbing.* God is calling you to a place greater than where you are.

Loving others is not always easy, especially when people hurt you. But God is love. And He empowers us to love others the way we ought to.

He will help us love like we've never been disappointed.

He will help us love like we've never let each other down.

He will help us love like we've never been hurt.

He will help us love like we've never been betrayed.

## Opposition Leads to Opportunity

I said at the beginning of this book that being offended is something you are going to experience in life. Jesus taught us, "It is impossible that no offenses should come, but woe to him through whom they do come!" (Luke 17:1 NKJV).

Offenses are inevitable. No one is exempt. One way or another, we are all going to get offended, get hurt, get insulted, get betrayed, get cheated, get shamed, get violated or lose our pride.

Since being offended is a biblical fact, we must learn how to deal with it.

I was in New Zealand a few years back. Saying it is a beautiful country is an understatement. As I was going for a run one morning, I couldn't help but admire the turquoise skies that stretched for miles and the glistening waters that shimmered like diamonds.

Suddenly, I noticed something. I did not see any birds flying. All the ones I saw were grounded. I would approach a swarm of birds chirping and hopping along the sandy path, and they would scramble out of my way without taking flight.

I mentioned this to a friend I was visiting at the time. What he said was fascinating. New Zealand is home to more species of flightless birds than anywhere else in the world. In fact, over half of all birds in this country cannot fly. The reason is that they have no predators. Before humans inhabited this island environment, no predatory mammals existed here. The main threats were other birds, like eagles and falcons. Flying came at a great cost to birds, so, over time, they stayed on the ground.[4]

Where you have no need to fly, you lose your ability to fly.

Some of us look at opposition as a bad thing. And certainly, it can feel that way. But opposition can be an opportunity. Think of it this way—without the opposition of offenses, you will never mount up with wings like an eagle (see Isaiah 40:31). Without opposition, you will never soar. You can scratch around in the barnyard, or you can fly—but not without opposition.

> **Without the opposition of offenses, you will never mount up with wings like an eagle.**

Opposition can cause you to face things and do things you could not have done, had you not had the opposition. Opposition will make you pray. Opposition will make you come running to God. Opposition will make you increase your faith.

You may need to start seeing those who offend or hurt you as an opportunity for God to take you higher.

You have read this book. You have heard God speaking to you through these words.

This material has probably dredged up old wounds, painful memories, reminders of a broken relationship. You may feel as though these things have caused you to flatline. But you have been looking for a chance to change. You know something needs to be done.

It's time to restart your heart.

Right now, the Holy Spirit is pulling into your driveway. He is coming for you. He is swooping into your home with a defibrillator. Charging the paddles with resurrection power, God is ready to press them down on your heart and shock you back to life. He is ready to revive whoever has been dead to you. He is ready to resuscitate your marriage. He is ready to resuscitate your family. He is ready to resuscitate your spirit.

It is time to restart your heart.

Friend, you may be in a raging storm, but God knew years ago that you would be where you are right now. Trust Him. He has already prepared the way for you. God can use the most trying of circumstances to fortify the walls of your marriage, your family and your relationship with Him.

> **God can use the most trying of circumstances to fortify the walls of your marriage, your family and your relationship with Him.**

Galatians 6:9 tells us, "So let's not get tired of doing what is good. At just the right time we will reap a harvest of blessing if we don't give up."

Don't give up just yet. "I am sure of this, that he who began a good work in you will bring it to completion at the day of Jesus Christ" (Philippians 1:6 ESV). God's grace is sufficient for the situation you are in.

Keep standing. Keep fighting. God will bring you through.

So try again.

Talk again.

Forgive again.

Reach out again.

Share a meal again.

Keep praying.

Keep believing.

Allow God to restart your heart. And start to love like you've never been hurt.

# NOTES

## Introduction

1. Mark Twain, *The Tragedy of Pudd'nhead Wilson* (Hartford, Conn.: American Publishing Company, 1900), http://twain.lib.virginia.edu/wilson /facsimile/pwchap16f.html.

## Chapter 3: It Is Never Wrong to Love

1. "10 Leading Causes of Death by Age Group, United States—2015," National Center for Injury Prevention and Control, Centers for Disease Control and Prevention, accessed July 13, 2017, https://www.cdc.gov/injury/wisqars /pdf/leading_causes_of_death_by_age_group_2015-a.pdf.

2. Mark L. Hatzenbuehler, "The Social Environment and Suicide Attempts in Lesbian, Gay, and Bisexual Youth," *Pediatrics* 127, no. 5 (2011), http://pediatrics .aappublications.org/content/early/2011/04/18/peds.2010-3020.

## Chapter 4: Stop Keeping Score and Start Losing Count

1. C. S. Lewis, *Mere Christianity* (New York: HarperOne, 2017), 115.

2. "Frequently Asked Questions: What's the Best Way to Get Heinz Ketchup out of the Iconic Glass Bottle?" H. J. Heinz Company, accessed July 13, 2017, http://heinz.custhelp.com/app/answers/detail/a_id/3502/related/1.

3. "Learning To Forgive May Improve Well-Being," *ScienceDaily*, January 4, 2008, www.sciencedaily.com/releases/2008/01/080104122807.htm.

4. Mayo Clinic Staff, "Forgiveness: Letting Go of Grudges and Bitterness," *Healthy Lifestyle: Adult Health*, November 11, 2014, http://www.mayoclinic .org/healthy-lifestyle/adult-health/in-depth/forgiveness/art-20047692.

5. Xue Zheng, Ryan Fehr, Kenneth Tai, Jayanth Narayanan, and Michele J. Gelfand, "The Unburdening Effects of Forgiveness: Effects on Slant Perception

and Jumping Height," *Social Psychological and Personality Science* 6, no. 4 (2014), https://pdfs.semanticscholar.org/2e0c/27023bad7762d24c79d9942144 62403f3cd4.pdf.

6. Corrie ten Boom, *Tramp for the Lord* (New York: Berkley, 2002), 192.

7. Ibid., 49–51.

## Chapter 7: Fighters, Fire Starters and Peacemakers

1. Benjamin Franklin, *The Art of Virtue* (New York: Skyhorse Publishing, 2012), front cover.

## Chapter 9: Fight for Your Marriage

1. Dr. Holly Hein, *Sexual Detours* (New York: St. Martin's, 2000), 77.

2. Pew Research Center, "The Gender Gap in Religion around the World" (demographic study), March 22, 2016, http://www.pewforum.org/2016/03/22 /the-gender-gap-in-religion-around-the-world/.

## Chapter 10: A Foundation That Lasts

1. Rome Neal, "Official End of Legendary Feud," *CBS News*, June 13, 2003, http://www.cbsnews.com/news/official-end-of-legendary-feud/.

2. Robertson McQuilkin, "Living by Vows," *Christianity Today*, February 1, 2004, http://www.christianitytoday.com/ct/2004/februaryweb-only /2-9-11.0.html?start=4.

3. Jim Priest, "Unforgettable Love Helps Couple Endure," *The Oklahoman*, April 9, 2000, http://newsok.com/article/2693121.

## Chapter 11: Fight for Your Family

1. Robert Edsel, *The Monuments Men* (Nashville: Center Street, 2010), 81.

2. Thomas Carlyle, *Sartor Resartus*, vol. 11 of *The World's Classics* (London: Grant Richards, 1902), 167.

## Chapter 12: Love God Like You've Never Been Hurt

1. Chris Fuchs, "After Three Decades, This Fortune Cookie Writer Is Passing the Baton," *NBC News*, December 22, 2016, http://www.nbcnews .com/news/asian-america/after-three-decades-fortune-cookie-writer-passing -baton-n697831.

2. Michelle Kim, "Meet the Guy Who Writes Your Fortune in Your Fortune Cookie," *CNN*, August 2, 2016, http://www.cnn.com/2016/08/02/us/fortune -cookie-writer-wonton-food-company/.

## Chapter 13: Keep Climbing

1. Avi Shlaim, "The Declaration That Changed History Forever," *The Guardian*, June 27, 2009, https://www.theguardian.com/books/2009/jun/28/balfour-and-weizmann-geoffrey-lewis.

2. Greg Asimakoupoulos, "Cheering the Invisible Victory," *Preaching Today*, accessed September 6, 2017, http://www.preachingtoday.com/illustrations/1998/july/4466.html.

## Chapter 14: The King Has One More Move

1. Marcus Luttrell, *Lone Survivor: The Eyewitness Account of Operation Redwing and the Lost Heroes of SEAL Team 10* (Boston: Little, Brown and Company, 2007), 102.

2. Ibid., 7.

3. G.R.F., "Anecdote of Paul Morphy," *Columbia Chess Chronicle* 3, no. 7–8 (August 18, 1888): 60. (More can be read about this story and the painting that inspired it at http://www.one-more-move-chess-art.com/One-More-Move.html.)

4. Kerry-Jayne Wilson, "Land Birds—Overview: 3. Flightless Land Birds," *Te Ara, the Encyclopedia of New Zealand*, September 24, 2007, revised April 20, 2015, https://teara.govt.nz/en/land-birds-overview/page-3.

**Jentezen Franklin** is the senior pastor of Free Chapel, a multi-campus church. Each week his television program, *Kingdom Connection*, is broadcast on major networks all over the world. A *New York Times* bestselling author, Jentezen has written eight books, including the groundbreaking *Fasting* and *Right People, Right Place, Right Plan*.

With a passion to serve others and foster unity, Jentezen was awarded the Martin Luther King Jr. Mantle of Destiny Award for his work and efforts for racial reconciliation. Jentezen has served as an advisor to CEOs and business leaders of multiple organizations and is listed among notable alumni at Barton College in Wilson, North Carolina. Additionally, he has served on an advisory board to the president of the United States.

Jentezen and his wife, Cherise, have been married thirty years. They have five children and two grandchildren and make their home in Gainesville, Georgia.

# Go Deeper into This Life-Changing Teaching!

Ideal for small groups, Bible studies and church classes, this 6-week study includes a copy of the book, a DVD with an in-depth video from Pastor Jentezen for each session, a participant's guide to take each member deeper into biblical truth, and a bonus downloadable leader's guide.

Discover answers to difficult questions such as *Why should I trust again?* and *How can I ever really forgive?* as you discover the tools and inspiration you need to see hope, receive healing, work through your wounds, repair damaged relationships and learn to love as if you've never been hurt.

*Love Like You've Never Been Hurt Curriculum Kit*
*Love Like You've Never Been Hurt Participant's Guide*
*Love Like You've Never Been Hurt DVD*

## ✓Chosen